Santa Fe

Lawrence W. Cheek
Photography by Eduardo Fuss

COMPASS AMERICAN GUIDES
An Imprint of Fodor's Travel Publications, Inc.

Santa Fe
Second Edition

LIBRARY OF CONGRESS CATALOGING-IN-PUBLICATION DATA
Cheek, Lawrence W., 1948–
Santa Fe/by Lawrence W. Cheek; photography by Eduardo Fuss.—2nd. ed.
p. cm. —(Compass American Guides)
Includes bibliographical references (p.) and index.
ISBN 0-679033-89-0 (alk. paper): $18.95
1. Santa Fe (N.M.)—Guidebooks. I. Fuss, Eduardo, 1938—
II. Title III. Series: Compass American Guides. (Series)
F 804. S23C48 1997 97-6759
917.89'560453-dc21 CIP

Editors: Kit Duane, Deborah Dunn, Barry Parr   Designers: Christopher Burt, David Hurst
Managing Editor: Kit Duane   Photography Editor: Christopher Burt
Map Design: Mark Stroud, Moon Street Cartography   Typesetting: Deborah Dunn

Compass American Guides, 5332 College Avenue, Suite 201, Oakland, CA 94618
Production House: Twin Age Ltd., Hong Kong   Printed in China
10 9 8 7 6 5 4 3 2 1

The Publisher gratefully acknowledges the following institutions and individuals for the use of their photographs and/or illustrations on the following pages: **Lawrence Cheek** pp. 85 (top), 124, 161; **George H. H. Huey** pp. 25, 26, 27; **Museum of New Mexico Photo Archives** pp. 24, 36, 39, 41, 46, 52, 53, 54, 56, 58, 60, 77, 101, 104, 105, 115, 123, 152, 175, 217; **Fine Arts Museum, Museum of New Mexico** pp. 106-107; **The Anschutz Collection, Denver** p. 128; **The Art Institute of Chicago, Alfred Stieglitz Collection** p. 74; **Boston Museum of Fine Arts, Gift of William H. Lane Foundation** p. 75; **The Motherhouse of the Sisters of Loretto Archives** p. 114; **Underwood Photo Archives, San Francisco** pp. 33, 37, 141, 154-155 (all), 179, 188-189, 190, 221; **Santa Fe Opera** p. 94. Photos on pp. 228-234 are courtesy of the hotels pictured.

We would also like to thank the following individuals for their contributions to this book: **Candace Coar** for proofreading, **Mary Jean Cook** for her piece on la doña Tules, **Arthur Olivas** of the Museum of New Mexico photo archives for his assistance supplying the archival illustrations, **Orlando Romero** for his expert reading, and **Nancy Zimmerman** for her editorial comments. Also thanks to **John O'Brien** from Atalaya Restaurant & Bakery and **Donna Pierce** from the Palace of the Governors.

*To Ann Aceves, whose grace, generosity,
and intelligence illuminate Santa Fe.*

C O N T E N T S

Topical Essays

Literary Extracts

Maps

ACKNOWLEDGMENTS

I have worked as a journalist in Texas, New Mexico, Arizona, California, Iowa, Mexico, China, and Russia—a fairly odd geographical patchwork; never mind why—but of all these places, the people of New Mexico were by far the most receptive, helpful, patient, ingratiating, and just plain friendly. They rewarded my curiosity about their land and their lives with mountains of information and many good stories.

First, many thanks to the staff of the Santa Fe Public Library, which granted me a borrower's card during my temporary residency and dredged up scores of volumes from the basement archives. Librarians even came to my study table from time to time, bearing books or articles I had overlooked. I've never encountered a more user-friendly library anywhere.

Susan Hazen-Hammond, a great friend and writer of two excellent books on Santa Fe herself, read several chapters, saved me from some errors, and offered many valuable suggestions. Help me thank her; buy her books.

Lynn Wood, a Tucson schoolteacher, neighbor, and great friend, divided up dozens of niggling research questions and fact-checking with me during the several days he spent with me in Santa Fe.

Most of my best insights into Santa Fe and places nearby came from interviews and informal conversation with natives. They include friend and hiking buddy Ann Aceves, Lesli Allison of St. John's College, artist Mary Brown, Truchas weaver Harry Cordova, Ray Dewey of Dewey Galleries Ltd., Judy Dwyer of Palace Avenue Books, William Franke of Hand Artes Gallery in Truchas, architect Michael Freeman, Santa Fe Mayor Debbie Jaramillo, Katherine Kagel of Cafe Pasqual's, Richard Myers of Agape Southwest Pueblo Pottery in Albuquerque, Taos author John Nichols, John O'Brien of Atalaya Restaurant & Bakery, historian Orlando Romero, Pamela Roy of the Santa Fe Farmers Market, James Rutherford of Copeland Rutherford Fine Arts, Ltd., archaeologist Curtis Schaafsma, fruit vendor/artist Loretta Valdez, orchard magician Euralia Vigil, adobe builder Robert Vigil, and Los Alamos mathematician/writer Larry Winter.

Finally, thanks most of all to Patty Cheek, nurse, musician, wife, and friend, who endured long months of separation while I worked in Santa Fe and even more months of the customary writer's angst and surliness as the book took shape. Only her care, affection, and advice made it possible.

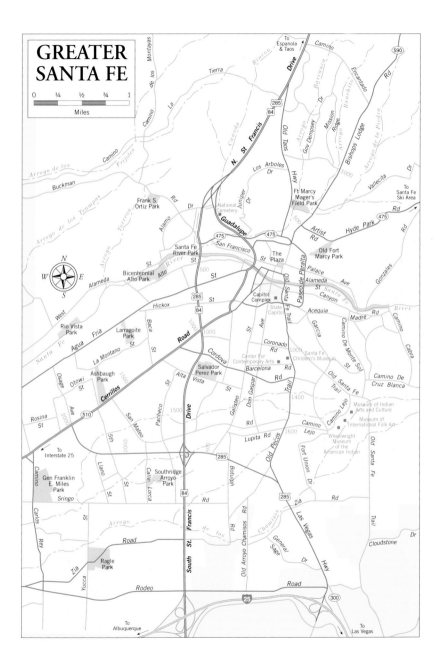

GREATER SANTA FE

0   ¼   ½   ¾   1

Miles

Santa Fe Facts

BASICS: *Santa Fe*
NAME DERIVATION: Spanish for "Holy Faith"
FOUNDED: 1607–1610
DESIGNATED CAPITAL OF NEW MEXICO: 1610
ELEVATION: 7,000 feet
POPULATION: 70,000

ETHNIC COMPOSITION

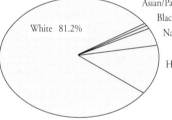

White 81.2%

Asian/Pacific 0.6%
Black 0.6%
Native American 2.2%

Hispanic 47.4% *

**Population of Hispanic origin is an
ethnic grouping and not additive to
the population racial groupings*

CLIMATE

Hottest Day	Coldest Day	Heaviest Rainfall	Heaviest Snowfall
99° F	-18° F	3.61 inches	16 inches
June 26, 1994	Jan. 13, 1963	July 26, 1968	Nov. 23, 1986

Population Growth

Year	Population	
1790	2,542	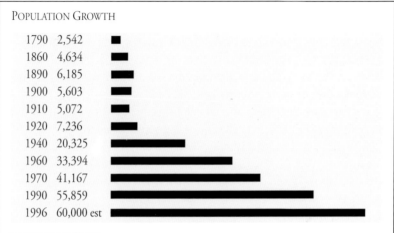
1860	4,634	
1890	6,185	
1900	5,603	
1910	5,072	
1920	7,236	
1940	20,325	
1960	33,394	
1970	41,167	
1990	55,859	
1996	60,000 est	

Interesting Facts

- Santa Fe is the oldest capital city in what is now the United States. The official founding date is 1610, but evidence records 1607 as the true founding.

The oldest house in the United States is reputed to be in Santa Fe.

- Santa Fe annually receives an average of 10 more inches of snow than Barrow, Alaska but also averages 300 days of sunshine.

- The oldest road in the USA runs from Santa Fe to Chihuahua, Mexico. It first served travelers in 1581. It is now Interstate 25.

- Chaco Canyon is the site of the world's largest excavated pre-Columbian Indian ruins.

- For over 200 years, Santa Fe was the administrative center for Spain's northern territories which stretched west to the Pacific Ocean.

- The *Places Rated Almanac* lists Santa Fe as the best metro area in North America for dining out (ratio of quality restaurants to population).

SANTA FE ❖ FANTA SE

I AM WAITING IN THE CHECKOUT LINE AT KAUNE'S, a cramped but tony gourmet grocery across Paseo Peralta from the New Mexico state capitol. I think I've seen the clerk before at a competing store. I ask.

"I actually work three jobs," she admits. "Two days here, three at Jewel Osco, and another day at an architect's office filing and keeping books."

"Sounds like a typical Santa Fe story," I say. "Work three jobs so you can afford to live here."

"No," she sighs. "I work three jobs and I *can't* afford to live here."

❖

Three blocks from my $800-a-month studio apartment is an intriguing sign: PROJECT TIBET. I wander into the courtyard that promises the project's headquarters, wondering what connection Santa Fe might have to Tibet. Inside are three rooms of exotic and lovely Tibetan crafts for sale—rugs, earrings, teapots, Buddha statues—and a cluttered office where Paljor Thondup, who fled Chinese-occupied

Santa Fe seems an unlikely location for this Tibetan Buddhist center, but in fact the city's setting seems to inspire spirituality.

The San Francisco de Asís Church of Ranchos de Taos inspired one of Georgia O'Keeffe's most important works of art.

Tibet in 1959, has struggled for the last 15 years to help fellow Tibetan refugees resettle in free countries.

"Why Santa Fe?"

"I came here 18 years ago to go to the College of Santa Fe. I decided to stay and start this project because Santa Fe is a unique place. It's a multicultural community, and that creates a meeting of minds."

"Also," Thondup adds, smiling gently, "we're easy to find here. More people drop in because of our sign on Canyon Road and ask about Tibet than ever would in New York, where there are seven million people who never talk to each other."

❖

This is not a conventional guidebook to Santa Fe. This is the work of a visiting journalist who has had a 20-year-long relationship with her, flitting among love, fascination, amazement, aggravation, and exasperation. This is a guidebook in which no subject is out of bounds, one in which Santa Feans talk to each other—and to me, about their lives and their histories and their dreams.

La Villa de Santa Feé (its original Spanish name), founded in 1607, claims more history, more fascinating characters, more art, and more multicultural energy than any other city in America with the possible exception of New York, which is more than 100 times Santa Fe's size. Santa Fe sports an unusual climate: two basic seasons, summer and winter, neither too extreme, with an interlude of autumn color that almost rivals New England's. It has three colleges, including a thoroughly unconventional one whose president unashamedly proclaims: "We don't know much about the twentieth century." It is the most concentrated art center in the world: retail sales by galleries and artists in 1993 rang up $212 million—pretty decent for a town of 60,000. In the decade past, Santa Fe style (for better or worse) captured the imagination of the whole nation, inspiring crafts, furniture, and architecture designed in an "antiqued" eighteenth-century Spanish Colonial dress. It is one of the culinary capitals of America, perhaps the only one save New Orleans that has evolved a broad and distinctive regional menu of its own. Anyone for crab and mango on tortilla spaghetti with habanero chile sour cream? (I did not, could not, make this up.)

This menu entrée, courtesy of a prestigious Santa Fe hotel kitchen, brings up the exasperating side of Santa Fe today. The city can be pretentious, outrageously expensive, and it ain't what it used to be.

Downtown, which appears on the surface to be one of the few lively city centers left in the country, is really naught but tourists until dusk—locals just don't go there because they can't afford anything in the stores, and they couldn't find a parking place anyway. The spiritual heart of Santa Fe's unique aesthetic, its adobe architecture, has been seriously corrupted—at least 80 percent of the modern houses in town are thrown up with 2 x 6 studs and chicken wire and stuccoed to masquerade as adobe, and they sell for a quarter-million up. New adobe houses start around half a million.

Although real estate slumped in 1995, the median sale price of a home was still a stunning $173,000, and historic houses bear price tags from another planet. Example: *Historical territorial 2BR, 2 bath, exquisite detailing, 12-ft. ceilings, pine floors, designer kitchen, walled private yard. Great location. $349,000.* Nobody in Santa Fe earns that kind of money; prospective buyers for such houses made their fortunes elsewhere.

Yet the old, uneven brown town is ineffably alluring. Sweep into Santa Fe on I-25 from Albuquerque (stay on the freeway until the Old Pecos Trail exit; avoid Cerrillos Road) and you'll see the last city in North America that truly embraces its natural environment. Almost nothing man-made save the cathedral and neighboring Loretto Chapel rises more than three stories to scrape the sapphire New Mexico sky. Houses and even commercial buildings snore under a quieting blanket of foliage. Even where the adobe is faked, the muted brown colors help connect the architecture to mother earth.

Or is it the other way around? As Susan Hazen-Hammond observes in her delightfully wry book *Only in Santa Fe,* this is the only city in America where the more money you have, the more likely you are to live on a dirt road. Santa Feans love to indulge in simulated rusticity. (A common gibe, even among locals, is to call the city "Fanta Se.") Some critics deride its pretensions, but there is also a deep and honest desire to perpetuate the city's unique qualities.

This is an irrepressibly friendly city. Strangers out for morning walks routinely offer greetings to each other. On one of my walks, a light drizzle had started, and a stranger in a car—a woman, amazingly—offered a ride. The young family that owned my apartment, correctly suspecting that I might be lonely 500 miles away from my own family at Thanksgiving, invited me to spend the holiday with them. This is the cultural landscape of Santa Fe.

That landscape comprises many different cultures including Indian, Hispanic, and Anglo. This is even more important to the textural richness of the city than its architecture and art. The cultures all depend on each other, and interact where they need to, but remain to a large extent distinct. There are race and class tensions in Santa Fe, as in every diverse community, and they grow as the chasm widens between rich and poor.

Whatever their cultural heritage, Santa Feans are fiercely in love with their city and the stunning land around it. They will endure any economic hardship in order to live with it. So will visitors. There are, however, many ideas in this book for saving money, something important to most of us.

The other side of the coin of friendliness is contentiousness. Santa Feans fight furiously over their city's present and past, and it frequently plays like theater of the absurd. City Hall operates like a third-world government, rife with nepotism and creaky bureaucracy. One homeowner was denied a permit to demolish a chicken coop on his property; the city deemed it a "historic structure." A telling local joke: How many Santa Feans does it take to change a light bulb? Six: One to screw it in and five to mill around and bitch about how much better they liked the

(following pages) A winter sunset highlights the Sangre de Cristo (Blood of Christ) Mountains looming above the town of Santa Fe.

OLD DAYS WERE BETTER FOR SANTA FE

*W*hen I first moved to Santa Fe [1957] it was so quiet on the plaza you could hear a rooster crow at the Delgado house on Palace Avenue, now headquarters for Banquest, which isn't a catering outfit as you might suspect but a quarter-of-a-billion-dollar bank holding company.

When I first moved to Santa Fe there was a San Ildefonso Indian named Joe who got paid five dollars a day for just sitting in the lobby of the Desert Inn, providing atmosphere for tourists. Joe would condescend to have coffee with me if I bought him some apple pie à la mode. We talked about growing Indian corn and how you could make Sears linoleum tile look like turquoise in jewelry.

When I first moved to Santa Fe cutting down billboards on Saturday night was a big social event, the only haciendas of consequence were built over three or four or more generations without the help of architects or regulated by city planners and building codes, and Fiesta was a family event with Dr. Deforrest Lord and his wife doing their handmade puppet show in La Fonda's lobby.

If you had a party you didn't have to think about what to serve; you just naturally cooked up some beans and posole and served that with both green and red chile stew or you asked Mrs. Delgado to put you on her list for three or four dozen tamales.

When I first moved to Santa Fe, us Anglos knew our place.

But Santa Fe has changed. Now we have instant haciendas costing a million or more and we have a Fiesta that is still a spectacle but it isn't OUR spectacle, so it doesn't amount to much and I suppose that those imported caterers will run Mrs. Delgado out of business.

The people I feel sorriest for are not the oldtimers who remember how it was but the newcomers who missed it all and I particularly feel sorry for those people at *People* magazine who can't find anything genuine to write about so they make a bunch of lies, calling Santa Fe a Shangri-la. Privately, we always thought it was Shangri-la but no one would ever dream of calling it that for fear of Santa Fe becoming something other than what it was meant to be, like another Disneyland with tour buses, wall-to-wall tourists, fast food chains and a plaza that exudes all the charm of a carnival midway.

Viva la Sagebrush Shangri-la.

—Lewis Thompson,
Letter to the editor in the *Santa Fe New Mexican*,
August 27, 1982

old one. As several Santa Fe residents told me, this sort of thing makes great copy (and even *The New Yorker* has gleefully reported on Santa Fe's local controversies)—but it's a little tiring to live with, year after year.

The *Santa Fe New Mexican,* the city's paper, bursts with letters daily decrying Santa Fe's allegedly fading uniqueness. Debbie Jaramillo, the city's mayor, told me with her usual frankness that the place has changed since she was a girl, and not for the better. "Growing up here it was almost like a third-world country: passive, a great mix of people, a tomorrow-is-just-another-day attitude. Today, it seems so hurried, fast-paced, people just figuring how they can make another dollar." Every Santa Fean who doesn't wring a living from the tourist industry is aching to crank back the clock.

They have their point, the cranky conservatives. Santa Fe was more charming 30 years ago. But in compensation, it is vastly more sophisticated today, and has much more to offer the visitor. Whatever you do, don't plan on spending just two or three days here. The city, the surrounding Indian pueblos, Spanish colonial towns, Taos, Anasazi ruins, mountains, canyons, gorges, skiing, fishing, hiking, river rafting, grazing those *habanero* sour cream sauces—Santa Fe asks for a month.

A *month* at Santa Fe's prices? Well, my one-room apartment sounded exorbitant indeed at $800, but that works out to $26.66 a night, it was a 15-minute walk from the Plaza, and it had a TV and foot-thick honest adobe walls. I was living near the heart of the most fascinating small city in America, working hours long enough that it might as well have been three jobs, and having a pretty damned good time.

> *I'm in love with Santa Fe;*
> *Like it better every day;*
> *But I wonder, every minute,*
> *How the folks who aren't in it,*
> *Ever stand it, any way,*
> *Not to be in Santa Fe.*
>
> —Mae Peregrine, Santa Fe, 1915

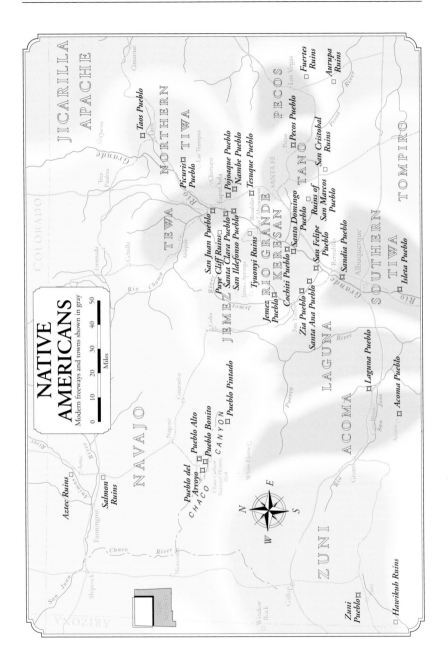

FIRST NEW MEXICANS

NEW MEXICO IS REDOLENT WITH HISTORY; we all know that. But New Mexico's prehistoric past swirls also in mystery.

A few years back, a visitor from Arizona was stretched out in a sleeping bag at Chaco Canyon, the strange nexus of the northwestern New Mexico Anasazi in the eleventh century. Shortly before dawn, he awoke with a bizarre and terrifying image exploding in his head.

"I had this very strong feeling that there had been sacrifices at some ancient time *right here,*" he said. "And then I started hyperventilating. I couldn't breathe normally. I thought I was having a heart attack."

He woke his wife, and she rushed him to the nearest emergency room, 90 miles distant. The doctors ran an EKG and found nothing wrong. Finally, after blowing into a paper bag he calmed down.

After he described that frightening morning, I told him something I had uncovered in my years of research on the Anasazi: A few archaeologists argue that they practiced ritual sacrifice, and if they had, Chaco Canyon would have been the obvious ceremonial center for it.

He stared at me, blood draining from his face. "I didn't know any of that," he said.

■ HUNTERS, GATHERERS, FARMERS, SPIRITS

At least 575 generations of people have lived in northern New Mexico—11,500 years of continuous occupation.

Archaeologists call the earliest people "Paleo-Indians" and know almost nothing about them except that they were nomads who hunted bison with lances equipped with spearheads of finely fluted and sharpened stone. By around 5000 B.C., the climate had become drier, the surviving bison plodded north in search of greener pastures, and a new culture of plant-gatherers now called the Archaic moved in. Or perhaps the Paleo-Indians just shrugged, changed their diet, and became the Archaic. Archaeologists don't know much about them, either.

Southwestern prehistory starts becoming interesting around 300 B.C., when corn, probably brought by itinerant traders from southern Mexico, began to be

Petroglyphs left by the first New Mexicans may be found in several areas of northern New Mexico, such as these in the Galisteo Basin south of Santa Fe.

cultivated. It was the most profound event in New Mexico's entire history, at least until the arrival of the Spaniards. Agriculture led to permanent settlements, and that to pottery, architecture, town planning, government, and—who knows?—prehistoric bureaucrats and lawyers to make rules and settle disputes. The very pervasive and elaborate Pueblo Indian religion of today probably began to germinate along with these first seeds of corn, because people depending on the weather for successful crops would need allies in the spirit world.

The prehistoric builders who left the stunning ruins in northeastern New Mexico at Chaco Canyon are called the Anasazi. The word is Navajo, and often is blandly translated as "the ancient ones." The more accurate translation is also the more ominous one: "enemy ancestors." To this day, Navajos steeped in tribal tradition avoid the ruins, believing that irritable spirits still lurk about—a notion that my friend who had the weird encounter at Chaco certainly respects.

The early Anasazi, also known as "Basketmakers," lived in dismal pit houses with floors excavated about 20 inches below ground and a framework of poles, sticks, and mud mortar heaped overhead. Around A.D. 750, the first small pueblos of stone masonry began to appear. The Chacoan "great houses" followed in the tenth and eleventh centuries, and cliff dwellings in the thirteenth. Early archaeologists assumed, as do casual visitors today, that cliff dwellings were built for defense. Present-day archaeologists are not so sure. True, a cliff dwelling would be almost impossible to assault—but also easy to besiege. And if your aerie is hundreds of feet above your farm, how do you protect your crops from raiders? Possibly the cliff dwellers were simply defending themselves from wind, snow, and rain.

The ascent of Anasazi art closely paralleled the rise in architectural sophistication. Until around A.D. 700, all Anasazi pottery was undecorated plainware. Gradually painted designs began to appear, and by the 1100s the Anasazi were crafting pots, bowls, and mugs in astonishing variety and with dazzling skill. Elaborate turquoise, bone, and shell jewelry appeared, as did decorated clothing. There are beautifully preserved Anasazi sashes woven from dog hair with repeating diamond patterns that are as sophisticated as anything in Santa Fe boutiques today.

The exceptional skills of Anasazi masons can be appreciated at Pueblo Bonito in Chaco Canyon.

The Anasazi were not at all a monolithic culture; there were striking variations in their architecture, pottery, and clothing from place to place. They probably spoke several different languages. They occupied the adjoining corners of four of today's states: New Mexico, Colorado, Utah, and Arizona. And in the short breath of prehistoric time from A.D. 1250 to 1300, the Anasazi world dispersed—a phenomenon that popular writers like to call a "mystery," and one that archaeologists term the "abandonment."

There is no "mystery" about it. Overpopulation in what is mostly a high, semi-arid plateau had consumed the scarce natural resources. And tree-ring studies tell of a devastating drought that persisted from 1276 to 1299. By 1300, most of the Anasazi cliff dwellings were left to the spirits, and the survivors, apparently, were surging into New Mexico's Rio Grande Valley, where the region's most reliable river ran.

What happened then was "a great mix of people," in the words of Curtis Schaafsma, curator of anthropology for the Museum of New Mexico. There were Anasazi from the west, Mogollon from the south, possibly Sinagua, Salado, and Hohokam from Arizona—as well as native Puebloans who had occupied the valley since A.D. 600. All this would account for the babel of languages spoken in the Pueblos today—Keresan in Ácoma and Laguna, various dialects of Tanoan in Taos, Santa Clara, and Jémez; and Zuñi in Zuñi Pueblo. All these Puebloans are the direct descendants of the great migration to the Rio Grande Valley.

A rare example of a polychrome Salado pot dating from the fourteenth century. (photograph by George H. H. Huey)

(opposite) A girl of Taos Pueblo photographed by Edward S. Curtis in 1905. Today's Puebloans are descendants of the Anasazi. (Museum of New Mexico)

An Ancient Tradition in Pottery

Pottery makers of the Southwest have been experimenting with clays, slips, and forms, both useful and decorative, for about 1500 years. Designs common in the pots shown below are still part of the pottery tradition today.

Hohokam Pot

This sacaton red-on-buff style pot was found at Casa Grande National Monument in Arizona. Its sloping shoulders make it typical of this period of pottery-making among the Hohokam people. A.D. 1100.

Anasazi Pot and Bowl

Found at Canyon de Chelly in Arizona, the cooking pot to the right was made for everyday use by the Kayenta Anasazi. The corrugations are made by pinching coils of clay. The black-on-white bowl below was found at Mesa Verde in southwestern Colorado. It measures more than 13 inches in diameter. The Mesa Verde region was a major center of pottery manufacture. A.D. 500–1300.

SINAGUA BOWL

The redware bowl to the right was made by the paddle and anvil technique and was found near Flagstaff, Arizona. The Sinagua culture, whose name means "without water," flourished between A.D. 500–1450.

SALADO JAR WITH HANDLE

An unusual pottery type, found in the vicinity of Roosevelt Dam in central Arizona. Its linear design was applied after the piece was polished. A.D. 1150–1450.

EASTERN PUEBLO POT

This glazed pot was made in an Anasazi pueblo in the Rio Grande Valley in New Mexico between A.D. 1425 and 1475. It was probably used for storing food or water.

(all photographs by George H. H. Huey)

Beginning around 1250–1300, immense stone and adobe pueblos—some with 2,000 to 4,000 rooms for living and storage—arose in the valley. Santa Fe's City Hall rests atop one; it probably was abandoned just a few decades before the Spaniards arrived. "When you go into the adobe brick of the Palace of the Governors," says Schaafsma, "you find potsherds. I think they [the Spaniards] just went to this big pile of dirt for their adobe."

Given the modern examples of India, Yugoslavia, and Russia—for just a few—how is it that people from so many ethnic stocks could come and live together in an increasingly crowded valley? Well, nothing in Southwestern archaeology today is as likely to start a fight among authorities as the question of prehistoric warfare.

Joe S. Sando, a Jémez Pueblo Indian, wrote in *Pueblo Nations: Eight Centuries of Pueblo Indian History:* "There were guidelines for well-ordered living. What the Pueblos have now as an unwritten 'tribal code' was essentially in operation in ancient times, remembered and obeyed as though carved in stone. The code was respected, understood, and taught from generation to generation." The code, Sando explained simply, came from the Great Spirit.

"They *didn't* merge peacefully," Schaafsma contends. "Rock art in the Rio Grande Valley is jam-packed full of all kinds of warrior imagery. The idea of the 'peaceful pueblos' is something people made up because it sounded good. However, 'warfare' is too broad a term. 'Squabbling' probably describes it better. The fighting was more opportunistic than ritualized."

Archaeologists are sure to squabble about it for generations to come. Meanwhile, there are several fascinating Pueblo ruins within a comfortable drive of Santa Fe for the rest of us to explore. Listed below are four Anasazi ruins in the vicinity of Santa Fe. They are also listed and more fully described in the chapter "DAY TRIPS FROM SANTA FE," beginning on page 159.

Built in the eleventh century, Pueblo Bonito had between 600 and 800 rooms, making it the largest of the "great houses" at Chaco Canyon. This Anasazi site is considered by many the preeminent archaeological site in the United States.

■ CHACO CULTURE NATIONAL HISTORICAL PARK
An astounding number of ruins are to be found at Chaco Canyon: more than 2,000 prehistoric ruins including eleven major pueblos. The canyon's centerpiece, Pueblo Bonito, is startling in its enormity. Mostly built between A.D. 1030 and 1079, the pueblo once contained from 600 to 800 rooms. The Anasazis' sophisticated construction techniques are apparent at Chaco, one of the most significant archaeological sites in the United States. (Also see page 191.)
From Santa Fe take Interstate 25 south 41 miles to NM 44. Follow Highway 44 about 120 miles to the turnoff for County Road 7900 (3 miles east of Nageezi Trading Post), then drive south along NM 57 for 27 miles to Chaco Canyon; (505) 786-7014.

■ PUYE CLIFF DWELLINGS
Carved out of volcanic tuff, the dwellings sit atop a 200-foot cliff and extend a mile along the cliffside. The Anasazi are believed to have inhabited the village from around A.D. 1250 to the mid-1500s. Santa Clarans believe themselves to be their direct descendants. (Also see page 180.)
Travel north from Santa Fe along US 84/285 to Española. Take the south exit and make a left on to NM 30. Drive about three miles and then at the sign for Santa Clara Pueblo, turn west and follow the road about three miles. The entrance to the Puye Cliff Dwellings is to the right; (505) 753-7326.

■ BANDELIER NATIONAL MONUMENT
This astonishing spectacle of prehistoric dwellings and volcanic rock formations covers nearly 50 square miles. The Anasazi migrated here about 1150 and the tribe thrived for 400 years. Most of the inhabitants deserted the area by the 1600s. Seventy-five miles of trails lead to the cliff dwellings, ceremonial caves, and ancient pueblos. The largest pueblo is Tyuonyi, an oval-shaped structure encircling a large plaza. The construction took about a century, supposedly reaching 400 rooms on three levels at its peak. (Also see page 182.)
Approximately a one-hour drive from Santa Fe. Take US 84/285 north about 12 miles, then turn west on NM 502. At the junction with NM 4, continue 6 miles to the parking area. Follow one of the hiking trails to reach the ruins; (505) 672-3861.

The foundations of some of Pueblo Bonito's hundreds of chambers are exposed to the desert elements and tourists' eyes in Chaco Canyon.

■ PETROGLYPH NATIONAL MONUMENT

Preserves more than 15,000 Anasazi petroglyphs and other prehistoric images dating back 2,000 to 3,000 years. Most of the petroglyphs—depictions of birds, other animals, and humans—were left by Puebloans between A.D. 1300 and 1650. Three easy, self-guided trails. (Also see page 186.)

From Santa Fe take Interstate 25 south about 56 miles, then take Interstate 40 west to Coors Road exit north. Turn left on Atrisco Drive, which becomes Unser Blvd. The monument's visitor center is at 6900 Unser Blvd.; (505) 839-4429.

■ PUEBLO CULTURE

What occurred in the lives of the people living along the Rio Grande between the time the Anasazi abandoned their cliff dwellings and the Spanish arrived 250 years later is inevitably a matter of speculation. Presumably, Anasazi people came down from the drier canyonlands to live along the Rio Grande, integrating their lives with those of others already there. The landscape the Anasazi had come from was one of deep fertile canyons, where rocks suitable for use in masonry buildings

La Fajada Butte in Chaco Canyon is typical of the region's desert scenery.

In 1975, a NASA astrophysicist examined petroglyphs depicting a supernova which exploded in A.D. 1054 and created the crab nebula. The petroglyphs were found in the village of the Great Kivas near Zuñi Pueblo. The cross above the crescent moon apparently represents the explosion. (Underwood Archives, San Francisco)

were many. Between Santa Fe and Taos, the landscape was wide open to the sky. The tributaries to the Rio Grande along which people came to live—the Taos, Santa Cruz, Pojoaque, Santa Fe, and Galisteo—dried up for months at a time, and in the spring, when they flooded with snowmelt, the waters ran red. The villages that grew up beside them were made not of rock (as were the Anasazis') or shrubs (as were those of earlier inhabitants in this area) but of dribbled mud in connected rooms, sometimes on several levels.

In looks, these were short, lean people, with dark eyes and hair and brown skin well adapted to blazing sunlight at high elevations. In warm months, children went naked, women walked barefoot, and men wore breechcloths. In colder weather people wore moccasins; men, kilts about their waists and cloaks of turkey feathers or rabbit fur. Some wore on their ankles little copper bells and beads made far to the south in what is now Mexico. Women wrapped themselves in pieces of cloth, four to five feet long and three feet wide, worn under the left arm and over the right shoulder and held together with decorated belts.

Within Pueblo villages, all aspects of life were carefully prescribed and ruled by the power of tradition. Rituals governed the tasks of planting, hunting, and building, and the emotional dramas of birth and death. If one fear was pervasive, it was the fear of witches, witches responsible for the mystifying events that intervened even in the most carefully ordered lives. People wanted to avoid being the subject of a witch's spell, and most likely, they wanted to avoid being identified as witches themselves. Witches were killed, and at times, groups of people were wiped out in purges.

All members of a pueblo owned the village and land in common, but families were granted plots of land on which to grow crops for their own use, as well as a room to live in. They were small rooms, reached by a ladder from the ceiling and made comfortable by mats of native cotton and yucca fiber woven on looms, and by stools made from cottonwood trunks. A new husband joined his wife in her family's room or rooms; if he left his wife, an ex-husband returned to his mother or sister.

Life outside the family was organized around the duties of cults and secret societies, to which men belonged by heredity and women joined through marriage. Each society was obligated to undertake particular civic duties, and its ceremonies took place in a large, usually round chamber, or *kiva*.

Ceremonial kiva *at Bandelier National Monument near Los Alamos.*

This was an enclosed, and for the most part harmonious, world. Evidence of networking with other cultures came in the form of trade goods that moved along ancient trade routes all over the Southwest and Mexico. Indian traders brought seashells from oceans, copper bells and macaw feathers from Mexico, and news from desert pueblos to the west —those of the Zuñi, Hopi, or Ácoma. Yet with the exception of nomadic warrior people who trekked down from the north and the west, occasionally attacking their villages, the citizens of these faraway worlds remained in place. Seasons came and went, the rivers ran full or sank into the sand, the villages prayed for rain and crops. When

The interior of a kiva, *scene of religious ceremonies.*

dawn brightened the horizon, the sounds and movements of creek water, children whispering a childish version of a familiar tongue, the sound of wind in the cottonwoods, of a dog barking and a owl hooting one last time, were all known parts of a familiar world.

Then, sometime in the year 1540, the Puebloans along the rivers between what is now Santa Fe and Taos heard rumors that a group of men had arrived near the pueblos to the west, in the desert. These men rode enormous animals and dressed in shining clothes that arrows couldn't pierce. When people went to do battle with these men, they raised sticks that killed with noises and fire. This was a scouting party sent by Gen. Francisco Vásquez de Coronado under the command of Capt. Hernando de Alvarado and accompanied by a chaplain, 16 cavalrymen, and four foot soldiers.

The group was coming toward what is now known as north-central New Mexico with the encouragement of the Viceroy of Mexico, whose ultimate allegiance, like theirs, was to His Most Catholic Majesty, King Carlos I of Spain.

Much has been written about the devastating effect this incursion had on the Puebloans along the river; what is perhaps more remarkable, is that they still exist and maintain a traditional, viable, and artistic culture. Between Santa Fe and Taos is a cluster of eight pueblos consisting of both ruins and modern villages. These pueblos, listed below, are described more fully in "EIGHT NORTHERN PUEBLOS."

- Tesuque
- Pojoaque
- Nambé
- San Ildefonso

- Santa Clara
- San Juan
- Picurís
- Taos

Ácoma Pueblo (described under "DAY TRIPS FROM SANTA FE," page 159) is one of several pueblos southwest of Santa Fe. Visitors to all pueblos should remember that these are quiet, traditional villages, where people want to go about their daily lives in peace without intrusive scrutiny.

Frontier photographer Edward S. Curtis took the photograph opposite while visiting Ácoma Pueblo in 1904. (Museum of New Mexico) Another early photo (above) captures a moment in the life of Picurís Pueblo. (Underwood Archives, San Francisco)

HISPANIC SANTA FE

THE SPANISH PROVINCIAL CAPITAL OF Santa Fe was conceived of imperialist ambition and born in conflict between church and state. Its adolescence consisted of more than two centuries of skirmishes, revolts, sieges, wars, executions, persecutions, ethnic divisions, and, for good measure, random violence.

No American city has a richer history; few have been surrounded by more tragedy and turmoil. The streets of twentieth-century Santa Fe, generally peaceful and lined with glittering galleries and boutiques, deceive. The full story is worth knowing.

The recorded history of New Mexico began in the summer of 1540, when part of an expeditionary army led by Francisco Vásquez de Coronado mustered across the present-day Arizona border along the Zuñi River. Coronado, the governor of New Galicia, then the northernmost province of New Spain, was a mere 30 years old. His monumental foray was spurred by rumors of the fabled Seven Cities of Cíbola, the cities of gold, a legend whose roots resonated deep into medieval Spain and originally had nothing to do with the New World. His recruits were mostly teenagers and men younger than himself who had grown up in privileged families and then had found themselves instantly impoverished by the draconian inheritance laws of Spain: everything went to the first-born son. These later-born were easily seduced by visions of wealth for the taking.

Coronado's expedition set the stage for the next hundred years. He had firm orders from the viceroy of New Spain to treat the Indians he encountered "as if they were Spaniards"—in other words, with decency and dignity. But how could his party follow this mandate when they were essentially searching for plunder—and incidentally, were determined to harness the barbarians to the yoke of Roman Catholicism?

Each time they entered a pueblo, the Spaniards would fire their guns and read the *requerimiento,* a proclamation claiming the village *en nombre del rey*—"in the name of the king of Spain." Furthermore, those who lived in the towns were ordered to consent to the teachings of the Church. If they refused, the proclamation continued, "We shall forcefully enter your country and make war against you in all ways and manners that we can. . . and the deaths and losses which shall accrue from this are your fault. . . ." Since these men were the first Spaniards the Indians had ever seen, the proclamation might as well have been read to them in classical Greek as in Spanish. But they quickly came to understand the Spaniards' intentions.

On July 7, 1540, Coronado's advance guard approached the Zuñi pueblo of Hawikuh. Rumors had it that this was one of the fabled Cities of Cíbola. What the Spaniards saw was a unprepossessing huddle of houses made of rocks and mud. Still, they demanded the village surrender in the name of their king and God. The Zuñis answered with a hail of arrows. The Spaniards followed with their crossbows and muskets and took what was to them a worthless pueblo by force. Many of the defenders were killed.

Coronado's band passed within a few miles of present-day Santa Fe, wandered as far as Kansas in a futile search for gold, and finally slunk back to Mexico in disgrace. Coronado himself was charged with abuse of the Pueblo Indians—at Tiguex, near present-day Albuquerque, the Spaniards had burned 30 rebellious Indians alive at the stake—but eventually he was acquitted.

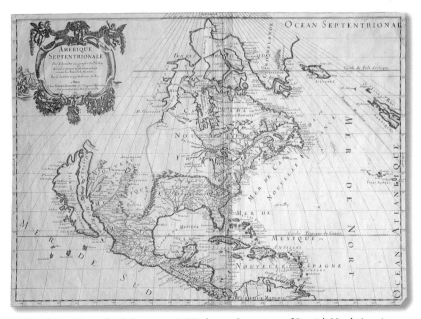

A French map drawn by G. Samson in 1669 depicts the territory of Spanish North America and shows the Rio Grande flowing into the Pacific Ocean just east of the island of California, rather than into the Gulf of Mexico. (Museum of New Mexico)

■ History Timeline ■

ca. 1150–1325 Pueblo Indian villages thrive along the Rio Grande.

ca. 1415–1425 Santa Fe region suffers worst drought in 1,000 years; many pueblos abandoned.

1540 Francisco Vásquez de Coronado comes upon Zuñi Pueblo in search of the Seven Cities of Cíbola.

1598 Under the leadership of Spanish explorer Juan de Oñate the first permanent European colony in New Mexico (the second in the United States) is established at San Juan Pueblo.

1607–1610 Don Pedro de Peralta names La Villa de Santa Feé (the City of the Holy Faith) as capital of the new colony. Construction begins on the Palace of the Governors.

1617 A Spanish priest, the first European settler in Taos, builds the Mission Church near the centuries-old Taos Pueblo.

1680 Pueblo Indians revolt against Spanish rule and colonists are exiled to what is now Ciudad Juarez, Mexico, across the river from El Paso.

1692 Don Diego de Vargas recaptures Santa Fe for Spain.

1792 Spain acquires the Louisiana territory and commissions Pedro de Vial to blaze a trail between St. Louis and Santa Fe. New Mexicans are forbidden to trade with anyone other than Mexico or its colonies.

1806 American explorer Captain Zebulon Pike, celebrated for his daring expeditions up the Arkansas River and along the Río del Norte, is captured and taken to Spanish Santa Fe.

1821 Mexico secedes from Spain. The following year American William Becknell opens the Santa Fe Trail and brings wagon loads of Northeastern goods to the residents of Santa Fe.

1846 General Stephen Watts Kearny leads the Army of the West into the Santa Fe Plaza and proclaims New Mexico U.S. territory.

1848 Treaty of Guadalupe Hidalgo cedes New Mexico to the United States.

1851 Jean Baptiste Lamy arrives in Santa Fe.

1862 The Confederate Army of New Mexico captures Santa Fe on March 10; Union forces retake the capital on April 8.

1869 Work begins on St. Francis Cathedral and is completed 17 years later.

1878   Lew Wallace is appointed governor and two years later, while still in office, completes an epic romance novel set in ancient Rome, *Ben-Hur.*

1880   The railway reaches Santa Fe. Streetlights are put up in the Plaza and the main streets. Billy the Kid spends the night in Santa Fe's jail.

1881   The telephone is brought to Santa Fe.

1912   New Mexico becomes the 47th state.

1915   Ernest Blumenschein, Robert Henri, Joseph Henry Sharp, and Bert Geer Phillips, among others, form the Taos Society of Artists.

1922   D. H. Lawrence and his wife, Frieda, arrive in Taos.

1929   Mabel Dodge Luhan invites Georgia O'Keeffe to New Mexico.

1945   The first atomic bomb is developed in secret laboratories at Los Alamos.

1956   Swiss emigré Ernie Blake builds Taos Ski Valley.

1957   John Crosby, 30, founds Santa Fe Opera; first production is Puccini's *Madame Butterfly.*

1967   The New Buffalo Commune, one of the first hippie communes in the nation, is founded in Taos.

1987   King Juan Carlos I is the first Spanish king ever to visit the former colonial capital of Spain.

Arrival of a caravan at Santa Fe in 1844. The opening of the Santa Fe Trail in 1822 signaled the beginning of the Anglo period in the region. (Museum of New Mexico)

■ EARLY SANTA FE

The first group of Spanish settlers to arrive in northern New Mexico came in 1598 under the leadership of Gov. Juan de Oñate. Among them were 130 families, 270 single men, and 11 Franciscan friars, along with 7,000 head of cattle and 83 wagons and carts. After enduring incredible hardships in the Chihuahuan Desert as they traveled north from Mexico, they settled along the Rio Grande near San Juan Pueblo. Soon the settlement was embroiled in disputes, and by 1610, Governor Oñate had been replaced by a new governor. The original settlers regrouped and joined with newly arrived colonists led by Gov. Pedro de Peralta to build a villa on the Rio Santa Fe. Six districts and a block for government buildings were marked out. Residents elected four councilmen, two of whom were to act as judges.

Within a few years, the villa of Santa Fe was a fortress-like compound, with arsenals, a jail, a chapel, and governor's offices. Two interior plazas were joined by outer walls, and entry was gained through a single gate with a trench in front of it. Settlers lived outside the gate and were given two lots for a house and garden, fields in which to plant vegetables, vineyards, and olive groves, and another 133 acres of land. In return they agreed to live in the area for 10 consecutive years.

In 1612, a Franciscan friar named Isidro Ordóñez rumbled into Santa Fe with a contingent of missionaries and a letter from the viceroy authorizing him to take charge of the New Mexican missions. The secular governor, Peralta, correctly felt that his authority was being challenged.

In less than a year, the friction boiled into real trouble. Just before a Sunday Mass in 1613, Ordóñez ordered Peralta's honorific governor's chair placed outside the church. When Peralta arrived he was furious and brought it back in. Ordóñez excommunicated him. Later that week Peralta ordered the priest out of town. When Ordóñez refused, the governor whipped out his pistolet and fired. Ordóñez was only grazed, but he vowed revenge. Ordóñez organized a posse and arrested Peralta, imprisoning him first at Sandía Pueblo, then at Zia. Eventually the Inquisition in Mexico City reprimanded Ordóñez and vindicated Peralta, but neither man ever returned to his post. For decades to follow, governors and priests in the little capital village would swap threats, excommunications, and arrests.

There was also trouble between church and state over the treatment of the Indians. The colonists saw a human resource to be exploited, extracting tribute in the form of bushels of corn and animal skins from the Puebloans and sometimes forcing

KINGDOM'S CAPITAL

S even leagues west of the aforesaid pueblo is the town of Santa Fé, capital of this kingdom. There reside the governors and the Spaniards, who number about two hundred and fifty, although for lack of weapons only fifty can be armed. Though they are few and poorly equipped, God has always enabled them to come forth victorious and has instilled into the Indians such a fear of them and of their harquebuses that at the mere mention of a Spaniard's coming to their pueblos they run away. In order to keep them in constant fear, they deal very severely with them whenever occasion arises for punishing a rebellious pueblo. . . .When I arrived there as custos, I started the construction of the church and friary, which—to the honor and glory of God—would merit admiration anywhere. There the friars are already teaching the Spaniards and Indians to read, write, play musical instruments, sing, and to practice all the arts of the civilized society.

—Fray Alonso de Benavides, *Memorial of 1630*

them to "donate" labor. Europeans also passed along the many diseases they suffered from themselves, which devastated the Pueblo population. This greatly vexed the church, which was losing potential converts—and tithes. It was hard, though, to say that the church was any kinder and gentler than the colonists. In 1675, four Tewa Indians were hanged as "sorcerers" after charges that they had "bewitched" the local priest.

Yet most of the priests were men of dedication and energy. By 1625, 26 friars had built 50 churches in New Mexico, and in their own era they were considered idealists with a highly respectable vocation. Franciscans left for the New World convinced they represented the only salvation available to man, in a form sanctified by God. In this they were backed by the religious training of their childhood and their years of seminary education. The severe discipline and punishment they meted out to the Indians paralleled what the Spanish Inquisition was visiting upon Spanish citizens at home.

As early as 1650 the Puebloans began mumbling of revolt against the unwelcome Europeans. (Potential revolutionaries were hanged, too, whenever the Spaniards could find them.) In 1680, the war finally commenced, and with a vengeance. A Tewa warrior named Popé sent messengers to all the pueblos carrying a cord of yucca fiber, tied with knots to remind them how many days were left

A Lady in the Wilderness, 1610

In 1598, Mexican-born explorer Juan de Oñate led an expedition of settlers and missionaries into northern New Mexico. Twelve years later several more Mexican families were sent to the settlement including Capt. Antonio Conde de Herrera and his wife Doña Francisca Galindo. Dona Francisca's wardrobe and household goods, listed below, represent the type of objects an upper-class colonial woman would have had during the early seventeenth century.

Doña Francisca's Dresses
- Two of brown and green cloth, trimmed
- One velvet adorned with velvet belts and gold clasps
- One black satin with silk gimps
- One black taffeta, trimmed
- One green coarse cloth with sashes embroidered in gold
- One crimson satin embroidered in gold
- One red satin with sashes and gold trimmings
- One tawny color with a white China embroidered skirt
- (Additionally) four ruffs

Doña Francisca's Household Goods
- Two pitchers
- Small pot and saltcellar of silver
- Six small and one large spoon
- One bedspread of crimson taffeta trimmed with lace
- Eight sheets
- Six pillows
- Three bolsters
- Two additional new pillows embroidered in silk of various colors

(Courtesy, The Palace of the Governors)

until the revolt. On August 11 the last knot disappeared and the storm began. The Puebloans killed most of the settlers outside Santa Fe and then laid siege to the Palace of the Governors, where a thousand defenders holed up. After days without water, the Spaniards decided they had to fight, even though they were badly outnumbered. At sunrise on August 20 they poured out of the Palace and successfully took back the town, killing 300 Indians in the process.

Still, the future looked bleak, and Governor Antonio Otermín decided to abandon the capital, at least temporarily. They retreated 300 miles south to El Paso del Norte (present-day Ciudad Juárez, Mexico). Of the 2,500 colonists and servants who joined in the retreat, 1,946 were recorded by the Spanish authorities as having arrived in El Paso, where they were to remain for a dozen years. In 1692 the governor-in-exile, Don Diego de Vargas, led an expedition to Santa Fe, found the Indians surprised and disorganized, and retook the capital without firing a shot. At Galisteo, Vargas's captain of artillery, Francisco Lucero de Godoy, found his young nephew, who had been held captive by the Puebloans since they had killed his family at their hacienda 13 years before.

Unfortunately, Vargas had to return to El Paso to collect the rest of his flock of settlers. When they set out again in October, almost 100 years after Oñate first brought treasure seekers and settlers to the region, most of those who followed were returning to the landscape of their childhood, where a parent, child, husband, or wife was buried. In all, there were 70 families, a contingent of soldiers, Indians from Mexico, convicts, lawyers, and chaplains. The group was supported by 18 wagons and three cannons, 1,000 mules, 2,000 horses, and 900 cattle. Their sacred object was *La Conquistadora,* a statue of the Virgin (now at St. Francis Cathedral). They made their arduous journey behind the imposing figure of Vargas, the son of a distinguished Spanish family, a tall man with dark eyes who wore his beard narrow and his hair long and carried with him in his saddle bag a full court dress.

When the colonists again arrived in Santa Fe in 1693 a battle ensued. Twenty-one Spaniards and 81 Puebloans died. Vargas reclaimed the village, but the cost had been high.

■ RESETTLEMENT

As the next century proceeded, the colonists whose farming and ranching supported the capital at Santa Fe scattered across the landscape of northern New Mexico. They had arrived with different motives than those of the conquistadors. They were looking for cultivatable land rather than gold, and they brought new varieties of beans, chiles, onions, oats, barley, wheat, peas, and melons, as well as chocolate and tomatoes. Their grazing animals spread out across the countryside, and their sheep provided wool to be spun and woven into cloth.

Family and community life were tightly structured, and deeply religious in their focus. Comanches occasionally poured down from the north on raiding parties—near Taos in 1760, 50 Spanish women and children were carried off and not seen again.

Feast days, Christmas celebrations, and weddings were the center of social life, as was shared work, like the yearly

Don Diego de Vargas, Governor of New Mexico from 1691 to 1697, came from an aristocratic Spanish family. (Museum of New Mexico)

cleaning of irrigation ditches. *Santeros* traveled from Santa Fe to the villages and haciendas, selling thin, large-eyed wood carvings of the saints to sanctify homes and fields. Men joined Penitente societies—lay religious fraternities—flagellating themselves to atone for Christ's suffering on the cross. The Church officially disapproved of these practices, causing the Penitentes to go underground. Another group the Church would have disapproved of were descendants of Spanish Jews who'd fled the Inquisition, ostensibly converted to Catholicism, and resettled in the kingdom's most far-flung outposts.

■ THE "MOURNFUL" CAPITAL

Eighteenth-century Santa Fe wore very little of the charm and élan that it began to acquire toward the end of the nineteenth. A famous description by visiting Friar Francisco Atanacio Domínguez, written in 1776, betrays the priest's disappointment at not finding much in the way of civilization:

*T*his villa . . . in the final analysis . . . lacks everything. Its appearance is mournful because not only are the houses of earth, but they are not adorned by any artifice of brush or construction. . . .

Although the population was small (the first census, in 1790, counted just 2,542),

THE POPULATION OF SANTA FE IN 1790

CATEGORY	MALE	PERCENT	FEMALE	PERCENT
Pure Spanish	820	67.38	875	66.04
mixed race				
Color quebrado	185	15.20	195	14.72
Mestizo	101	8.30	121	9.13
Mulato	42	3.45	43	3.25
Indian Servants	31	2.55	5	0.38
Indio	36	2.96	85	6.42
Coyote	2	0.16	1	0.08
Total Population	**1,217**		**1,325**	

De Yndio y Mestiza
Coyote.

urban sprawl was already a problem. As Domínguez went on to observe, most lived on "small ranches at various distances from one another, with no plan as to their location." The real problem was not aesthetics, but Apaches: without a garrison wall, the town could not be defended. In 1777 the new governor, Don Juan Bautista de Anza, devised a plan to rebuild the town compactly on the south side of the Santa Fe River, but was rebuffed by the ranchers, who wanted to stay close to guard their fields. According to New Mexican historian Marc Simmons, the ranchers actually worried more about bears prowling down from the Sangre de Cristo Mountains to poach in the fields than they did about Indian raids. (On rare occasions, bears still wander into Santa Fe today. One morning in 1994, a 250-pound black bear showed up just a few blocks from the government complex on Cerrillos Road. A state Game and Fish officer shot and killed it, prompting a furor that lasted for weeks.)

Other menaces of daily life included rattlesnakes, smallpox epidemics, floods, droughts, and shootings. There was little organized commerce; the 1790 census listed exactly one merchant. The reason was Santa Fe's isolation and the Crown's churlish prohibition against trade with any nation except Spain and her colonies. Trade with Mexico City was an arduous 1,400 miles away. Most goods were either handmade or bartered with Indians at trade fairs at distant Taos and Pecos.

The church, as always, managed to import at least some of the trappings of culture. Although adobe was the only building material available, the military chapel of 1760 called *La Castrense* showed off a stunningly intricate baroque *reredos* carved by stonemasons imported temporarily from Mexico. (The chapel is gone, but the *reredos* is the focal point of Cristo Rey Church today.)

The echoes of Santa Fe history still resonate in the city's character today, although with the waves of newcomers that character is rapidly being submerged. The hardship and isolation fostered a sense of fatalism, independence, and especially a stubborn pride in being a unique people. When a modern Santa Fean shouts a cranky epithet at the occupants of a luxury car with out-of-state plates, well, it's not very different from Santa Feans in 1777 telling carpetbagging Governor de Anza to go to hell with his plans for their town.

By 1800, foreigners—trappers, traders, and haphazard voyagers from abroad—began to arrive with increasing frequency on the borders of the Spanish frontier. They brought news of a changing outside world: the city of New Orleans, Spanish in 1800, reverted to French again in 1803, only to be sold to the 30-year-old United States. In 1805, nothing was more unnerving to the people of Santa Fe than an incomprehensible medical innovation: the Spanish government decided to vaccinate its people for smallpox. When the government doctor went through the city and out to pueblos and haciendas with his vials of fluid, Indian and Spanish parents were equally suspicious of his intentions.

Although periodic hostilities between the Puebloans and the Spaniards continued into the nineteenth century, the two gradually became allies in the face of Apache and Comanche raids. Eventually, they intermarried, the Indians learned Spanish, and many even returned to the Catholic Church. The Puebloan diet surely diversified with new foods introduced by the Europeans. And they didn't lose their traditional lands as did so many other Native American tribes. But Spanish rule still had been a tragedy of epic proportions. Historian Marc Simmons estimates that in 1540 the Puebloans had numbered 40,000 to 50,000 people; by 1700 they had dwindled to no more than 14,000. Today, however the population has climbed back up to nearly 40,000.

The reredos *of Cristo Rey Church.*

■ MEXICAN SANTA FE

The year of 1821 was the pivot point in the development of Santa Fe. It began 11 years earlier and thousands of miles away with the 57-year-old parish priest of Dolores, a poor Indian town 120 miles northwest of Mexico City. With the famous *grito de dolores,* still celebrated throughout Mexico and the American Southwest on September 16, the priest exhorted his people to break the bondage of Spain. "My children!" shouted Father Miguel Hidalgo y Costilla. "A new dispensation comes to us this day. Are you ready to receive it? Will you be free?" Eleven years and 600,000 deaths later, Mexico was an independent nation—and an immense one, because its territories included California, Arizona, New Mexico, and Texas, an area larger than today's Spain, France, Germany, Italy, Great Britain, Sweden, Norway, and Finland combined. From the southern tip of Mexico the empire stretched an incomprehensible 3,000 miles to the northern stub of California.

Becoming part of this empire was the best thing that had yet happened to Santa Fe. The Mexican government welcomed trade with the United States, and within a year a trapper and Indian fighter named William Becknell had begun to blaze a wagon trail from Independence, Missouri, 780 miles to Santa Fe. It was the first major trade route punching into what would soon become the American West.

There is an ironic footnote to Mexican independence in Santa Fe. A celebration was clearly in order, but the town's big cigars seemed not to know exactly what to do. So the *alcalde* (mayor) summoned one of the first American merchants to reach Santa Fe, one Thomas James, to ask what Americans might have done to welcome their own relatively recent independence. James suggested cutting the tallest pine they could find, stripping the branches, erecting it in the Plaza, and running up the flag. On February 5, 1822, as all Santa Fe gathered for the ceremony, James logically suggested the honor belonged to the governor, Facundo Melgares.

"Oh, do it yourself, Señor James," said Melgares. "You understand such things." So an American citizen raised the first Mexican flag over the New Mexican capital, launching five days of bacchanalia. The party might have been more subdued had a wise man been able to foretell the future: that in just 24 years New Mexico would have another new flag—as a Territory of the United States.

Carts pulled by lumbering mules and oxen brought tons of American and even European fabrics, clothing, building materials, tools, hardware, kitchenware, and booze along the Santa Fe Trail. But the wagons were in chronic danger of attack by

MEXICAN MANNERS

*T*he Mexicans, like the French, are remarkable for their politeness and suavity of manners. You cannot visit a friend but he assures you that, "*Está V. en su casa, y puede mandar,*" etc. (You are in your own house, and can command, etc.), or, "*Estoy enteramente á su disposicion*" (I am wholly at your disposal), without, however, meaning more than an expression of ordinary courtesy. Nor can you speak in commendation of any article, let its value be what it may, but the polite owner immediately replies, "*Tómelo, V. Señor; es suyo*" (Take it, sir; it is yours), without the slightest intention or expectation that you should take him at his word.—Mr. Poinsett observes, "Remember, when you take leave of a Spanish grandee, to bow as you leave the room, at the head of the stairs, where the host accompanies you; and after descending the first flight, turn round and you will see him expecting a third salutation, which he returns with great courtesy, and remains until you are out of sight; so that as you wind down the stairs, if you catch a glimpse of him, kiss your hand, and he will think you a most accomplished cavalier." Graphic as this short sketch is, it hardly describes the full measure of Mexican politeness; for in that country, when the visitor reaches the street, another tip of the hat, and another inclination of the head, will be expected by the attentive host, who gently waves, with his hand, a final '*á dios*' from a window.

—Josiah Gregg, *Commerce of the Prairies*, 1844

Indians, and the encounters were vicious. In 1828, Indians shot a Capt. John Means off his horse, and, according to one account, "scalped him before he had drawn his last breath." That same year a party of trappers invited the enemy to a parley, then fired on them, killing half a dozen Indians. Today, as we drive from Missouri to Santa Fe in a couple of days, risking no more than speeding tickets, it is hard to imagine the mixture of adventure, trepidation, and opportunity that swirled within these early dreamers.

The Americans who lumbered into Santa Fe encountered a culture that astounded them. For example, the Spanish women of Santa Fe routinely smoked, danced, and gambled in public; they owned their own businesses and even made small fortunes. Priests routinely and openly took mistresses.

The town was wide open to carousing, partying (for any imaginable excuse), drinking, and especially gambling. Yet, according to historian Janet Lecompte "courtesy was the first rule of conduct." Against that backdrop, many of the Americans proved to be boors. "They jeered at New Mexican folkways, broke up *fandangos* with drunken violence, and seduced and then abandoned both wives and children." Disparaging comments permeated the Anglos' impressions. Traveler Albert Pike in 1833 labeled the New Mexicans as "a lazy gossiping people, always lounging on their blankets and smoking cigarillos." Later in the century, Gen. William T. Sherman quipped that "The United States ought to declare war on Mexico and make it take back New Mexico."

SHAMEFUL

January 23, 1864:

We have heard of what we hope never will again occur in Santa Fe. It is, that at a fandango, a few evenings since, two of the females became insulted and enraged at each other, and that American men present endeavored to inflame the ill will and violence of the two women, the one against the other,

Dancing the fandango. *(Museum of New Mexico)*

and that a ring was formed and knives placed in the hands of each, for a desperate fight.

We hope no American will so far forget the dignity of human nature—his name and race, as to be found encouraging, again, such exhibition of passion and violence between two females who, but for being animated and excited by spectators, would restrain within decent bounds their personal animosities.

—News clipping from the *Santa Fe New Mexican* as reprinted in Oliver La Farge's
Santa Fe: The Autobiography of a Southwestern Town

LA PATRONA DE SANTA FE

Santa Fe once had a *patrona,* a godmother. Her name was Gertrudis Barceló, but she became famous as la Tules—the Tules. That name lingers today at the corner of Burro Alley, Palace and Grant avenues. And for a brief time, historic Burro Alley was called Calle Barcelona, for it was here that the gambling *sala* and residence of the notorious *monte* player dominated the social and gambling scene during the 1830s and 1840s.

Never in the history of this fandango-loving town has a woman entertained citizens and visitors with such intelligent wit and style. The legend of the expert *monte* dealer (*monte,* a card game of pure chance) has been depicted in park murals, told in novels, newspapers, and magazines, and portrayed in musicals and dramatic monologues. Her legend (somewhat embellished) grew even larger in 1844 with the publication of Josiah Gregg's famous epic of the Santa Fe Trail, *Commerce of the Prairies.*

La doña Tules, born around 1800 in Sonora, Mexico, of Catalan heritage, traveled with her family up the Rio Grande Valley along the centuries-old *El Camino Real de Tierra Adentro,* the Royal Road to the Interior. The Apache-infested road from central Mexico had been the route of New Mexico's first colonists led by don Juan de Oñate in 1598.

The Barceló family settled in the *Rio Abajo* (down-river) in the warm, wine-growing village of Valencia, south of today's Albuquerque. Here Tules married Manuel Antonio Sisneros and gave birth to two sons, both of whom died as infants. Motherhood

(continues)

Burro Alley in the 1890s. (Museum of New Mexico)

was the biological wealth coveted by the woman gambler whose name appears time and again in church records as a godmother to the children of her friends and family.

Despite the sexual license of early New Mexico, adultery was frowned upon and considered illegal. More than once la Tules defended her reputation against local rumors. Her neighbor had complained to the *alcalde* (mayor) of Tules illegally cohabiting with an Anglo. Taking the offensive, Tules demanded that the neighbor back down. The two women later signed an act of conciliation. Soon, however, Tules was again back in the *alcalde* court demanding an apology from another woman for unnamed slander.

La doña Tules.
(Museum of New Mexico)

Tules traveled long distances to gamble at trade fairs in Mexico and throughout New Mexico. But it was the political excitement and international flavor of Santa Fe that finally captured her. She attended *bailes* (balls) and dealt *monte* to fur trappers, soldiers, merchants, governors, generals, women, and even the local clergy. A $10,000 stake was not uncommon, and gamblers were known to have covered as much as $40,000 in a single bet.

Hard specie for use by the U.S. Army was in short supply at the beginning of the Mexican War in 1846. The erudite Lt. Col. David Dawson Mitchell, who was said to have made the ladies swoon as he walked the streets of St. Louis, needed money for supplies for his men to travel to Chihuahua. In public appreciation for a loan of $1,000 from la doña Tules, Mitchell escorted her on his arm to a play entitled "Pizarro," given in the old Palace of the Governors.

In January 1852, New Mexico's newly-appointed Bishop Jean Baptiste Lamy officiated at the funeral of the gambling doña. Tules paid the church and Lamy almost $2,000 to be buried in the Capilla de San José (a south chapel) of the *parroquia* (parish church), on the site of today's St. Francis Cathedral.

The *gente fina* of Santa Fe—Hispanic, Anglo, clergy, and military—attended the grand finale to the life of la doña Tules. In life she had achieved wealth and fame, and in death the unprecedented fortune to be the first woman in New Mexico history to be buried by a bishop who desperately needed money to restore his crumbling mud churches.

The subject of Bishop Lamy's homily was the importance of leading a good life. Had la Tules led that good life, her name might well have missed the pages of history.

—Mary Jean Cook

■ TAKING NEW MEXICO

Oh, what a joy to fight the dons
and wallop fat Armijo!
So clear the way to Santa Fe!
With that we all agree, O!

It was this cheerfully militant ditty that accompanied a band of 300 U.S. Army regulars and volunteers as they marched over the Santa Fe Trail from Missouri to New Mexico in 1846. The Americans were commanded by Brig. Gen. Stephen Watts Kearny, a renowned fighter and ardent patriot. Manuel Armijo, the New Mexican governor, had a reputation as a good governor, badgering Mexico City to serve the needs of distant New Mexico and constantly advocating something relatively rare in the province: literacy. But he must have felt himself between the proverbial rock and hard place when he heard that the United States had declared war on Mexico. Armijo was obligated to defend Santa Fe—which meant defending it against the Americans who were forming its prospering economy.

The priests, curiously, tried to whip up flames of resistance. They warned the New Mexicans that the Americans would destroy the churches, rape the women, and brand the men on the cheek, like cattle. At this news, many Santa Feans fled. Eventually, so did Armijo. Convinced he couldn't win, he loaded what he could into seven wagons and left the town. On August 18, 1846, Kearny and his ad hoc army captured the capital of New Mexico without spilling a drop of blood. As Historian Janet Lecompte described it:

> They met no opposition, only sullen faces and downcast eyes. The wail of women rose above the din of the horses' hooves. As cannons boomed, soldiers raised the American flag on a newly constructed pole in the plaza. One soldier wrote later that he saw black eyes peering from behind latticed windows, many filled with tears, but a few gleaming with joy. The moment held both despair and hope—sorrow that Santa Fe was no longer a loving child of Spain and Mexico, and anticipation that the United States would prove a more attentive parent.

JEAN BAPTISTE LAMY

On an August Sunday in 1851, a French-born priest named Jean Baptiste Lamy rode into Santa Fe to become the territorial capital's first bishop. His Spanish was abysmal, his health questionable, and he had no idea of the scorpions' nest of trouble he was about to ride into—or to create.

Born to a prosperous peasant family in a small French town, he had grown up on narrow, dusty streets and attended mass in an unexceptional provincial church. Of eleven brothers and sisters, he was one of four to survive to adulthood.

During his years in seminary, Lamy heard heroic stories of priests carrying the word of God into the new world. Inspired to join their ranks, he took orders, and at the age of 25 stepped aboard a sailing ship bound across the Atlantic from the port of Le Havre. During an uncomfortable voyage, he studied English and ate sparingly— the ship did not provide food to its passengers; they had to bring their own. Lamy arrived in New York after 44 days at sea, and he set out to meet with the bishop of Cincinnati, Ohio.

The controversial and energetic Bishop Jean Baptiste Lamy. (Museum of New Mexico)

The year was 1839, and the United States was in the midst of a depression. Lamy's bishop sent him into the Ohio forest to build a congregation and a church. His contemporaries were Abraham Lincoln, recently elected to the Illinois state legislature, and Robert E. Lee, who was working as an army engineer rechanneling the Mississippi river near St. Louis.

Lamy spent the next 11 years in parish work, first in Ohio and then in Kentucky, ministering to congregations, and most importantly buying land and designing and raising the money to build churches. He must have identified with his new country because in 1847 he became a citizen of the United States. He did, however, return to France the following year and on several other occasions, visiting family and trying to find priests willing to come with him to the new world.

In 1848, the United States signed treaties concluding its war with Mexico and annexing the American Southwest. Reports from U.S. soldiers about the questionable state of the church in New Mexico Territory weren't long in coming to the attention of the American Catholic Church, and letters on the subject of its improvement were soon being sent back and forth between Baltimore and Rome. Various people were suggested for a bishopric in the newly acquired territory, and in the summer of 1850, Father Lamy—at work building a church school in Covington, Kentucky—was suprised to hear that Pope Pius IX had named him bishop of Santa Fe.

Lamy returned to Cincinnati, then traveled by steamer down the Ohio and then onto the Mississippi River, bound for New

Bishop Lamy disapproved of santos carvings such as this when he arrived in Santa Fe.

Orleans on a boat that carried passengers, animals, cotton, and slaves for sale. Reaching the Gulf, he boarded a ship to travel west, and barely survived its wreck. But, survive he did, and he continued west on land toward Santa Fe—an arduous trip through arid country whose few cultivatable areas were suffering from a severe drought. In this territory of 70,000 people, he'd been told, there were 15 priests, of whom six were infirm with age.

Several thousand citizens of Santa Fe turned out to welcome him on a Sunday in the summer of 1851. Directly upon arriving, he went to say Mass in the old church of St. Francis, where the parishioners knelt on floors that were for the most part of mud-packed earth. Seemingly in honor of his arrival, clouds massed, and the rains came. Certainly an auspicious beginning; but the next day the vicar of Santa Fe told Lamy he refused to recognize him as a bishop, despite the papal bulls Lamy had in hand, because there'd been no word of such thing from the bishop in Durango, Mexico.

(continues)

❖ ❖ ❖

Willa Cather immortalized Lamy in her famous historical novel *Death Comes for the Archbishop,* published in 1927. But the real Lamy was more intriguing than the "brave, sensitive, courteous" and one-dimensional creature of Cather's creation.

You can begin to sense Lamy's character at the east end of San Francisco Street in downtown Santa Fe, where the great, gray Romanesque cathedral towers over the low, brown adobe town. This is Lamy's legacy. He conceived it, imported the architects and stonemasons for it, and had it built literally around the adobe parish church that had stood there before.

The Catholic Church that Bishop Lamy encountered in New Mexico was little better than pagan, he felt. One Santa Fe priest, Lamy discovered, was "keeping a very young and beautiful married woman in his house." When Lamy ordered her out, the padre essentially told his bishop to go to hell. In little more than a year, Lamy and the Spanish-speaking priests in his see were at war, and Lamy was still struggling to learn Spanish.

Lamy felt a moral obligation to rehabilitate the New Mexican church, but he never understood New Mexicans. He couldn't tolerate the primitive, sometimes

Sante Fe's Catholic cathedral dominates East San Francisco Street in this 1865 photo. (Museum of New Mexico)

macabre folk-art carvings of *santos* (saints) that inhabited the churches, and at one point ordered them thrown out.

Lamy's most controversial act was his excommunication of an elderly New Mexican priest, Padre Antonio José Martinez of Taos. Martinez was an intelligent and respected activist who had battled the practice of compulsory tithing to the church. Bishop Lamy, while he decried priestly greed and corruption, reinstated the tithe, cut the percentage paid to the priests, and increased the amount under his own control. He wasn't out for personal gain; nobody has ever accused him of that. He did dream of a French cathedral towering over Santa Fe.

Lamy appointed a Spanish friend, Don Damaso Taladrid, to replace Martinez. Martinez didn't budge and sent laundry lists of grievances to his bishop. Lamy didn't answer. In 1857 Lamy dispatched his vicar apostolate, Joseph Priest Machebeuf, to Taos to kick Martinez out of the church. But even after excommunication, Martinez maintained an independent, crypto-Catholic church with his own followers.

"Bishop Lamy's removal of the native clergy was tragic," writes historian Ray John de Aragon, voicing a common viewpoint among Hispanics. "It deprived the Hispanic New Mexicans of their leaders, leaving a 'wound that was long to heal and a scar that can still be felt.'" On the other hand, Lamy gave a great deal to Santa Fe at a pivotal moment in its development: he set up a school for boys in his own house and summoned the Sisters of Loretto to establish an academy for girls. Writes author Paul Horgan, "Affirmation was the theme of his life. Who knew how much spiritual energy was thoughtlessly inherited, absorbed, and reactivated in later inheritors?"

Arrogant, determined, and hard-working, kind in his own manner and unquestionably honest—this is the complex mosaic cobbled from different points of view. Maybe the best tribute to Jean Baptiste Lamy, as you watch the evening light paint his statue and cathedral, is to think of him as a complicated and contradictory figure.

ARRIVING IN SANTA FE

A few miles before reaching the [capital] city, the road again emerges into an open plain. Ascending a table ridge, we spied in an extended valley to the northwest, occasional groups of trees, skirted with verdant corn and wheat fields, with here and there a square block-like protuberance reared in the midst. A little further, and just ahead of us to the north, irregular clusters of the same opened to our view. "Oh, we are approaching the suburbs!" thought I, on perceiving the cornfields, and what I supposed to be brick-kilns scattered in every direction. These and other observations of the same nature becoming audible, a friend at my elbow said, "It is true those are heaps of unburnt bricks, nevertheless they are *houses*—this is the city of Santa Fé."

—Josiah Gregg, *Commerce of the Prairies,* 1844

A view of Santa Fe, circa 1846–47. (Museum of New Mexico)

CONTEMPORARY SANTA FE

SANTA FE HAS BEEN CASTING ITS MYSTERIOUS spell over visitors for more than a century. In 1880, the first locomotive huffed into town, bringing building materials and patients with tuberculosis or emphysema who prayed that the thin, dry air would cure them. Artists and tourists followed in growing waves. Between 1880 and 1900, the Anglo population of New Mexico quadrupled. Most of them fell in love with the place. Martha Summerhayes, a young army bride, rhapsodized in 1889:

> As we drove into the town, its appearance of placid content, its ancient buildings, its great trees, its clear air, its friendly, indolent-looking inhabitants, gave me a delightful feeling of home. A mysterious charm seemed to possess me. It was the spell which that old town loves to throw over the strangers who venture off the beaten track to come within her walls.

By 1900, Santa Fe was beginning to acquire a reputation as a colony of painters and writers, even though statehood was still a dozen years away and the entire population of the Territorial capital was about 5,000. "Santa Fe Style," far from being a fabrication of the 1980s, was being talked about as early as 1916. In that year an architect named William Templeton Johnson published a prescient article that advocated stripping the town of Victorian architectural influences, restoring the Plaza to its original dimensions (twice as large as we see it today), creating a linear river park, and designing a new federal building "in the *'Santa Fe' style* of architecture." Johnson correctly realized that Santa Fe's future lay in tourism; he only failed to predict the monster that it would become.

Santa Feans date the birth of the "monster" to the early 1980s, when a tsunami of national publicity rolled over the little city. In 1981, *U.S. News & World Report* called it "a new Palm Springs." *Newsweek* hailed it as "America's Salzburg." In prose shamelessly empurpled, *People* termed it a "Sagebrush Shangri-la. . . a mecca of mesas and margaritas." A little higher on the literary scale, *National Geographic* called it "an enchantress among cities without the Circean evil that turns men into swine." In 1992, readers of *Condé Nast Traveler* voted Santa Fe the *number one* destination in the *world*, beating out San Francisco, Vienna, Florence, Rome, Sydney, London, Paris, San Antonio, and Venice.

But the article that created the biggest local howl was a ten-page piece in the May 1981 *Esquire* that said, in effect, pack your BMW and move to Santa Fe:

> There is, quite simply, a *here* here, a surfeit of it. Art and music. Bookstores. Thousands of acres to hike, climb, fish and ride. Good bars and worthy restaurants, warm and friendly nearly every one. Lots of single people. Nifty things to buy and wear: cowboy boots, Stetsons with peacock feathers, down-filled vests.
>
> And there is an attitude in the air that some townspeople call tolerant, others laid-back, still others *mañana* [tomorrow]. Finally, there is a prevailing live and let live heritage, Santa Feans tell you, that promises privacy to the most hermitic, acceptance to the most eccentric. Imagine: all this set in a place as lovely as God could design. . . .

Not all the commentary was quite so breathlessly infatuated. In a funny and revealing 1982 *New Yorker* report about a raucous spat over a Santa Fe homeowner's roof design, author Calvin Trillin advanced the Theory of the Dumbest Sons:

> According to this theory, there was a time when a number of wealthy Eastern families assigned their dumbest son—the son who was of no use in the bank or the factory—to a life of coupon clipping in Santa Fe, and everything that has happened since can be traced to either the customs or the genes brought from the East by those founding offspring.

Turning slightly more serious, Trillin went on:

> Although the Theory of the Dumbest Sons has a simplicity that has always appealed to me, I suspect that a theory closer to the truth would be the Theory of the Sons or Daughters who Didn't Fit In—didn't fit in because of being uninterested in business or being artistic or sickly or eccentric or dumb or not dumb enough to devote their lives to a family bank. In northern New Mexico, they found a romantic setting inhabited by romantic people. . . .

Other commentators found no romance in Santa Fe. English writer John M. Taylor invented a whole new word to vilify the city's modern character: *boutiquery*.

> Wherever it appears, boutiquery is a sure sign of sterility; only the cause varies. In Santa Fe effete pretension supplants genuine creative impulse because the rugged scenery of northern New Mexico is overpowering.

Paradoxically, the vast and pitiless landscape that is all too real provokes a fussiness of response that is all too phony. Without scenery Santa Fe would scarcely exist, yet scenery on the grandest scale vitiates the town's existence. . . . the locals are willing enough that life among the mesas be mindless. . . .

Mindless? Contemporary Santa Fe can legitimately be indicted for vanity, excessive self-promotion, cutesy-poohing itself—but not with mindlessness. There are about 30 bookstores in town. There are three colleges. A typical week's lectures and meetings listed in *The New Mexican's* ¿Que Pasa? (What's happening?) includes some 40 options such as: Tibetan Buddhist meditation, a baroque recorder society, literacy volunteers, French, Spanish, and Portuguese conversation groups, the Santa Fe Green Party, "Zen and the Art of Making a Living," and a "Full Moon Ceremony: Meditations and teachings with Wild Horse Woman in the tradition of Grandfather Thundercloud." Something, surely, for every mind.

The small amount of bad pub flung at Santa Fe in the '80s hardly hurt it—it was the laudation that did the damage, turning Santa Fe into a place too expensive for most people to live. In the '90s, the city's Office of Community Development estimated that Santa Fe's "middle class" was evaporating at the rate of two percent every year. Nearly everyone thinks the city has grown too fast, and water is becoming a worry. In 1996, the city council ordered a 25 percent reduction in water use, enforced by colossal penalties: one resident who flouted conservation found a one-month bill for $6,659.

Resentment against newcomers is readily apparent. In the 1980s, a wave of wealthy Texans swamped Santa Fe; in the 1990s, came a flood of second-homers from California. A columnist for the *Santa Fe Reporter* who drove a borrowed car with California plates for a week wrote that she was hailed on the streets with invective and reproving sign language. Mayor Jaramillo said the new gated communities on the city's periphery have created tension: "Many old Santa Feans have told me when they look at these gates, 'why do I feel like I'm the stranger in this town?' " she said. Other long-time residents say the water issue separates the people who belong to Santa Fe from the interlopers. "If you grew up here, you understand this as a desert," one told me. "We would shower once a week, just before we went to confession." She said it wistfully, like a remembrance of halcyon days.

But halcyon days for Santa Fe developers seemed to peak in the early 1990s, and by mid-decade the bloom was off. In 1996, Santa Fe tumbled to number 12 on *Condé Nast's* list, the real estate balloon began to deflate, and the crowds on the

streets were visibly thinner. Merchants grumbled, but for other residents and visitors it seemed like a welcome step back from madness. In the fall of 1996, you could actually score a table in a good restaurant without a reservation.

It's just another cycle, and Santa Fe's allure has persisted through four centuries of stressful changes. Not even the most obdurate pessimist imagines that it will ever become an ordinary place. It is too resilient, too rich in history, in culture, in scenery for that.

Start with that scenery. Santa Fe stretches out on a valley between the majestic Sangre de Cristo ("Blood of Christ") and Jemez mountain ranges, the twin southern tails of the Rockies. The hills surrounding are decorated in sweet-scented piñon, juniper, and sage, which give way to towering ponderosa and aspen in the higher elevations. The sunlight is sharp yet somehow sensuous at the same time, giving an unusual definition to every leaf and limb rock. In Santa Fe, one's senses seem sharpened.

That goes for within the city, too. Cerrillos Road is as much a strip-zone eyesore as any major artery in Albuquerque or Tucson, but the compensation is a walk along the Santa Fe River Park (William Johnson's idea came true), or even the Acequia Madre, shaded by cottonwoods and American elm—surely the most romantic ditch in the country.

Santa Fe's man-made scenery is protected by one of the oldest historic district zoning ordinances in the country, first adopted in 1957. There are some 7,000 buildings in five historic districts, and any remodeling, or any new building, must be approved by the Historic Design Review Board. Originally, the ordinance said that everything in these districts had to conform to the Spanish-Pueblo or Territorial style. This led to some laughable architectural mongrels, such as the owner of a Victorian house being forced to graft a Pueblo Revival addition onto it. A 1992 revision made the ordinance more realistic, while still guaranteeing that the unique style of historic Santa Fe would be preserved.

Ah, Santa Fe Style. *Ristras* of red chiles hung by the front door. A cozy beehive fireplace in a corner of the living room. A Chimayó rug on the wall. Hand-painted pine cabinets, chairs, and table in the dining room. Kokopelli coffee mugs on the table. Like most superheated trends, Santa Fe Style eventually became a caricature of itself. It always was more a marketing scheme than an actual catalog of design or state of mind. Writer Carmella Padilla explained it beautifully in an analysis in *The Dallas Morning News,* examining products from Old Spice Santa Fe Men's Cologne to Pepperidge Farm's oatmeal-raisin Santa Fe Cookies. As Padilla

Making ristras, *the strands of chile peppers that have become a visual symbol of the Santa Fe area.*

St. John's College

It's called St. John's College, but "cloister" might be a better description. It is a fully accredited four-year liberal arts college, so outstanding that 80 percent of its graduates go on to law school, medical school, or graduate school, but in other respects it is not of this world.

I tell John Agresto, the president, that if I were a Martian anthropologist who had crashed onto St. John's Santa Fe campus and stumbled over his curriculum, I'd assume that Earth's twentieth century didn't matter much. "Well, I'll be honest about it," he replies. "We as a faculty don't know much about the twentieth century."

St. John's was founded in Annapolis, Maryland, in 1696 as King William School. The name was changed, for obvious reasons, during the American Revolution. In 1937, an administrative revolution overthrew the conventional liberal arts curriculum and replaced it with a unique program centered around the study of 200 "great books" of Western civilization, from Plato's *Republic* to Werner Heisenberg's *The Physical Principles of the Quantum Theory*. In 1964, St. John's opened a second campus in Santa Fe.

A more idyllic setting for a college would be hard to imagine. Its Santa Fe–style buildings step down the piñon-forested slope of Sun Mountain at the southeast edge of town. A man-made pond with a miniature waterfall gurgles fetchingly in the campus's plaza. But this isn't a place to kick off shoes, doze through the afternoon, and party through the night. Though grades are not emphasized, St. John's is tough.

Agresto describes how the students have to publicly defend their senior essays: "You wear a robe, the faculty members are in their academic gowns, you process into the room, the doors are locked and barred, and for one full hour—and it stops exactly when the hour is over, in mid-sentence if necessary—you are taken apart. There have been oral exams postponed three, four, or five times because of intense throwing up."

But at the same time, St. John's offers a gentle, nurturing, remarkably civilized environment for serious students. Most live in single rooms on campus. In class discussions they must address each other as "Mr." or "Ms." Professors, here called "tutors," never lecture; they sponsor discussions. Students are graded, but they don't learn their grades unless they go to the registrar and file a request. And those grades, Agresto says, are determined more by how thoughtfully they teach each other than how well they act like students.

St. John's is tough for the 60 faculty members, too. Every one, including President Agresto, has to be able to teach every course in the college, from classical Greek

---

(preceding pages) A hand-tinted photograph of a corner along Santa Fe Avenue captures a moment in time in the Santa Fe of today.

through Mozart's operas, Marx's economic theory to nuclear physics. All the faculty members teach—and every student takes—four years of geometry, calculus, astronomy, biology, and physics (in which twentieth-century texts *are* allowed).

St. John's rigorous and conservative curriculum has its critics. Agresto, the son of a Brooklyn bar owner, admits that the students could lighten up: "We're about to build a gymnasium, which I think we need. Sometimes you need to put the books down and throw a basketball around." And the twentieth century is still the future as far as St. John's is concerned. T. S. Eliot, Wallace Stevens, and Virginia Woolf have made guest appearances among the "great books," but haven't yet been seated in the curriculum. "The faculty fights about this all the time," Agresto says. "Some of this will find its way in, probably too late."

explained, quoting marketing gurus, Santa Fe came to represent the quintessential relaxed Southwestern lifestyle, while still suggesting urban sophistication.

Or what they *imagine* that life to be. Santa Fe author Susan Hazen-Hammond notes that "Santa Fe Style can mean Ph.Ds working as waitresses and former executives driving cabs, even when the rest of the U.S. economy is booming."

Surveying the streets of Santa Fe, the visitor would swear that current Santa Fe Style is a $55,000 Range Rover. But this is just common-sense prestige transportation. The reason so few wealthy locals own Lexuses or BMWs is that on snowy winter days they would be just so many immobile ice sculptures.

But there is a real Santa Fe Style, and it's not something that can be packaged and exported, hung on a wall or stuffed in a burrito.

Santa Fe Style was illustrated in a 1974 controversy over the commemorative obelisk in the Plaza that honored "the heroes who have fallen in the various battles with *savage* Indians in the territory of New Mexico." After nearly a year of furious debate, one August day a stranger calmly climbed over the low wrought iron fence around the memorial, chiseled out the offending adjective, and disappeared. End of problem.

Santa Fe Style *was* Municipal Court Judge Tom Fiorina's annual tradition of dismissing parking tickets on Thanksgiving week in exchange for turkeys donated to the needy (a tradition ended, alas, by higher judicial fiat in 1995).

It is an old Hispanic gentleman slowly wandering about St. Francis Cathedral, playing meandering tunes on a scratchy violin day after day. He bothers no one, and no one bothers him. It is the ceremonial autumn torching of Zozobra, a 40-foot-high effigy of Old Man Gloom. When the muslin, paper, and wood monster annually goes up in flames, the troubles and sorrows of Santa Feans symbolically

burn with him. It is a cold Christmas Eve on Canyon Road, with flickering farolitos outlining uneven parapets and dirt driveways, and 30,000 people strolling the street, sipping hot cider and singing carols. It is street names that evoke 400 years of real history—Paseo de Peralta, Calle de Anza—rather than a developer's Spanish rhapsodizing.

It is a soft Hispanic edge to the quality of life, like the unevenly rounded corners of an adobe house, that perseveres even after 400 years of tumultuous change. It is a tolerance of eccentricity left over from the days when Spanish women shocked gringo traders by their gambling, smoking, and entrepreneurship. Santa Fe never tolerated a puritan, and it mostly dodged the Victorian era, and the positive effects are still evident today. "There are enough good qualities left here," says Mayor Jaramillo, "that if we can protect them, we have something worth hanging onto."

Santa Fe, in the end, is much more than "mesas and margaritas." There is an ineffable spiritual quality about the place, something that changes people who come here even as they change her. What D. H. Lawrence wrote three-quarters of a century ago remains true today:

> *I* think New Mexico was the greatest experience from the outside world that I have ever had. It certainly changed me forever. . . The moment I saw the brilliant, proud morning shine high over the deserts of Santa Fe, something stood still in my soul, and I started to attend. . . In the magnificent fierce morning of New Mexico one sprang awake, a new part of the soul woke up suddenly, and the old world gave way to the new.

When the towering wooden and papier-mâché image of Zozobra (left) is burned every year, the troubles and sorrows of Santa Feans symbolically burn with him. At Christmastime the town's residents place farolitos *(above) along the city streets.*

ART AND MUSEUMS

IN A ONE-MILE, SEVERAL-HOUR WALK along Canyon Road, Santa Fe's gallery
ghetto, you could see and buy:

- Twelfth-century Anasazi pottery
- Nineteenth-century Sioux ceremonial moccasins
- Twentieth-century American bowling pins
- Native American prayer feather fetishes
- Contemporary American impressionist painting
- Contemporary American abstract expressionism
- Contemporary Russian painting
- Contemporary Czech furniture
- Handmade turquoise, silver, or gold jewelry
- Kinetic sculpture with neon lighting
- Tibetan Buddha sculptures
- Moose and mule-deer antler chandeliers
- Cowboy art
- Gay erotic nude cowboy art

And vastly more. The list could run on for pages. There are about 80 galleries
on Canyon Road, said to be the most concentrated art market on Earth—and
another 120 galleries sprinkled elsewhere around Santa Fe. You can choose
among a dozen openings every Friday night. You can discover fine art, kitsch, and
schlock, cheek to jowl. You can spend ten bucks or $100,000. This is also the
most democratic art market on Earth, eager to accommodate the whole spectrum
of taste and budget.

There is more music and theater in Santa Fe than in most American cities five
times its size. You can listen to a professional men's chorus perform in the acousti-
cally brilliant Loretto Chapel and then walk three blocks to the famous La Casa
Sena Cantina for a *carne adovada* burrito and a concert of Broadway tunes by professional singing waiters. There are several theater companies, including the Santa
Fe Community Theater, the oldest such group in New Mexico. *Pasatiempo*, the weekly arts and entertainment section published by the *Santa Fe New Mexican*, usually
runs 64 to 80 pages, bursting with previews, reviews, and features.

Northern New Mexico has been a fertile land for the arts for centuries. In the 1830s one churlish commentator sniffed that "There is no part of the civilized globe, perhaps, where the arts have been so much neglected." True, nobody was buying symphony tickets in Santa Fe in the 1830s—but neither were they anywhere else west of the Mississippi in that era. Although their nineteenth-century wares were clearly inferior, Pueblo Indians had been making distinguished painted pottery since the A.D. 700s. The Ortega family of Chimayó began weaving lovely woolen rugs in the late 1700s; its eighth generation continues today.

The modern blossoming of the arts in Santa Fe (and Taos) began more than a century ago. It started as a tentative trickle, a handful of painters and writers from the East coming out to visit the strange and exotic territory of New Mexico—and finding themselves utterly captivated. By the 1890s, there were art exhibits in the Palace of the Governors. By 1920, dozens of distinguished artists had made Santa Fe their home, and the isolated little town was becoming a major center in the avant-garde abstract expressionist movement. In 1929, Georgia O'Keeffe adopted nearby Abiquiu as her summer residence, and the course of her artistic life was forever changed. She wrote to a friend of her experiences:

> I have frozen in the mountains in rain and hail—and slept out under the stars—and cooked and burned on the desert. . . It has been like the wind and the sun. . . there doesnt seem to have been a crack of the waking day or night that wasnt full. . . .

What lured them were the same elements that are still attracting artists of all imaginable varieties: the land, the light, the people. One contemporary abstract painter in Santa Fe told me he is inspired by "the ferocity of the landscape." A jewelry artist, in contrast, said she derives inner peace from Santa Fe's natural environment. "If a piece hasn't gone well, or if someone's criticized my work, all I have to do is drive 10 minutes out of town, and the grandeur of this place really places everything in perspective. Human beings, in the grand scheme of things, aren't very damned important."

The light in northern New Mexico is unlike anyplace else in the country: intense and powerful but not harsh or punishing. The well-known expressionist landscape painter Marsden Hartley, who worked around Taos in 1918 and 1919, said that New Mexico "is not a country of light on things, but a country of things in light"—a wonderfully enlightening description.

And then there were the indigenous and Hispanic cultures that obviously provided many artists with fascinating subject matter, but also influenced others, even landscape painters and sculptors, in more subtle ways. Says James Rutherford, a Santa Fe gallery owner, "New Mexico became more of a mecca for the arts than other places in the Southwest: there's a blend of cultures here that doesn't quite exist anywhere else."

For a long time, Santa Fe was also an inexpensive place to live and work—an eternal concern of struggling artists. Gallery owner William Vincent, who moved to Santa Fe in 1956, reminisced in the *Santa Fe New Mexican* that "Back then, Canyon Road was loaded with artists. They lived there and painted there, and it wasn't high-priced at all."

Landscape No. 3, (Cash Entry Mines, New Mexico) *was painted by Marsden Hartley while he was living in Berlin in 1920, based upon his recollections of a visit to New Mexico in 1918 and 1919. (The Chicago Art Institute, Alfred Stieglitz Collection)*

Deer Skull with Pedernal, *painted in 1936 by artist Georgia O'Keeffe, New Mexico's most famed resident artist prior to her death in 1986. (Gift of the William H. Lane Foundation, courtesy Museum of Fine Arts, Boston)*

No more, for sure. Although Santa Fe is still loaded with artists, many have grown discouraged by the stratospheric cost of living. The result is that the artists' colony has dispersed, to some extent, and resettled in small towns nearby, such as Chimayó, Española, and Galisteo. "However, Santa Fe's economy is a blessing to artists as well as a curse," said Rutherford, "because while wealthy people are moving here and driving up the cost of housing, they're also buying art."

Perhaps because of this, the art scene in Santa Fe is more eclectic, adventurous, and vital than it was even ten years ago. Back then, art collectors could find themselves wearying of the commercialized sameness of much of the stuff in the galleries—paintings of aerodynamic Indians, pueblos in the sunset, weathered corrals capped with snow. "It was a tough place to show if you didn't do coyotes," one artist growled. Kitsch still abounds in Santa Fe, particularly in the downtown boutique galleries (where Kokopelli, the prehistoric rock-art figure of a hunchbacked flute player, has replaced the howling coyote as the ubiquitous decoration on everything from earrings to, incredibly, toilet paper holders). But the profusion of serious art in every medium from jewelry to monumental sculpture is amazing. One gallery, for example, recently hung a show of photographic portraits of Soviet women pilots who flew combat in World War II. Such an exhibit would have seemed very strange in the Santa Fe of a decade past.

"I would rank us among the top four art markets in the country, along with New York, Los Angeles, and Chicago," said downtown gallery owner Ray Dewey. "And I think we're more diverse than the others. We're very strong in realism, contemporary Indian art, Hispanic art, and regional art. And I think we have an undeserved reputation as an expensive art market. Sure, you can spend $1 million here. But you can also get something of real quality for $100 or $1,000. I think that's our greatest strength."

Shopping for art in Santa Fe can be both exhausting and exhilarating for the same reason—the sheer number of things to look at. Some suggestions:

Begin by picking up a few publications. *Wingspread Collector's Guide to Santa Fe–Taos,* published every two years, is a free glossy book packed with illustrated gallery ads and short features. A monthly magazine with the quirky name of *The* runs arts features and profiles. *Pasatiempo,* published every Friday in the *Santa Fe New Mexican,* is an entertaining and indispensable guide to all the arts in town.

Watch for notices of studio tours. Several times a year, groups of artists open dozens of their studios to visitors for a whole afternoon. It's an excellent way to get to know the artists and their work. Show openings, usually on Friday or Saturday nights and always announced in *Pasatiempo,* are convivial, informal, and not at all snobbish. Some feature cheap, but complimentary, jug chablis.

Don't quit looking at the Santa Fe or Taos city limits. Small galleries of remarkable variety and depth thrive in the small towns sprinkled around, and their prices sometimes are delectably low—they show unknown "emerging" artists and don't suffer downtown overhead. And don't neglect Albuquerque, a short 60-mile drive: its galleries are as lively as Santa Fe's.

As for museums, Santa Fe has several that display extraordinary work from the superb Museum of Indian Arts and Culture to the Museum of Fine Arts, near the plaza. See "Art Museums" in this chapter.

■ INDIAN ARTS

The modern era of Native American arts was foreshadowed by the railroad, on which the first locomotive hissed into Albuquerque in 1880. Until this, tourism in Santa Fe and everywhere in the Southwest was limited to itinerants and adventurers, few of whom had much interest in arts and crafts. But the railroads opened the territories to waves of families and settlers, and they were intrigued by the indigenous folk art.

Though by this time, New Mexican Indians hardly had art at all. Puebloan pottery in the late 1800s was a pale remnant of the Anasazi traditions of 600 years

María Martínez on the patio of the Palace of the Governors around 1920. (Museum of New Mexico)

earlier. Most of it was utilitarian and indifferently made. Few people could have imagined selling or buying it. In New Mexico, a San Ildefonso potter named María Martínez became the pivotal figure in not only the revival but the new blossoming of an ancient art. A modest woman who said she "never cared about being well-known or anything," María and her husband Julian began making pots for the tourist trade in the early 1900s. María would build the pots, not on a wheel, but in the classic manner of coiling snakes of moist clay into the pot's rough shape, then scraping it smooth and finally polishing it with a "slip" or skin of fine clay. Julian, a self-taught but gifted designer, would then apply the paint. In 1918 an experiment produced a whole new kind of pottery—matte black designs on a gloss black background—and it made both artistic and commercial history. In a few years, several potters in San Ildefonso were making a living in black-on-black ceramics, and the other Rio Grande pueblos, sensing at last an opportunity to lift themselves from the mire of poverty, began to develop distinctive styles of their own.

Pueblo pottery today is a highly developed art form, intricate and expressive, constantly evolving far from its utilitarian roots. Any good Pueblo pot is still formed in the laborious, time-honored coil-and-scrape fashion. This is important not merely for tradition's sake. Hand-forming a bowl or pot gives it a humane, slightly imperfect architecture (like an adobe building) that provides a welcome retreat from the anonymity of machine production: the artist's character lives in the work.

Anita Suazo, a Santa Clara potter, displays one of her works.

CLASSIC SOUTHWEST JEWELRY

COCHITI PUEBLO
SILVER SQUASH BLOSSOM NECKLACE

Traditional squash blossom necklaces feature side pendants in the shape of a squash or pumpkin flower. In this necklace from Cochiti Pueblo, 25 miles west of Santa Fe, the squash blossoms have been replaced with crosses; this particular design has a double-barred cross with a heartlike bottom, resembling the Catholic sacred heart and the Indian dragonfly that in many Pueblo cultures was the symbol for water.

ZUÑI BRACELET

The Zuñi Pueblo, the largest pueblo in New Mexico, is located due west of Albuquerque near the Arizona border. For centuries, Zuñis traded turquoise to Plains Indians for buffalo hides and to Mexican tribes for parrot plumes. Over the years the Zuñi have become famous for their extraordinary work in turquoise and silver as exemplified above in this huge, sunburst-design, cluster bracelet. Circa 1930.

NAVAJO CONCHA BELTS

The idea for concha belts derived from disk-shaped hair ornaments sold to Plains Indians by white traders as early as 1750. Navajos linked hair ornaments to form decorative belts, impressing into the silver Mexican designs. Circa 1885.

Buyers new to the art of Pueblo pottery sometimes don't catch on. "It's the hardest thing for them to deal with, if they don't know how the pots are made," said Albuquerque dealer Richard Myers. "They can't rationalize paying $1,000 for something that's got a flaw in it."

$1,000? Yes, easily. Fine Pueblo pottery is expensive. The price depends partly on size, partly on quality, mostly on the artist's reputation. And it may not help to bypass the city galleries and buy direct from the potters in the Pueblos: they know what the retail price should be, that's what they sell it for, and cheerfully pocket the markup themselves.

Many other Indian arts have thrived in this century, particularly painting, sculpture and jewelry—and along with them have thrived the artists.

The annual Indian Market, staged in the Santa Fe Plaza every summer since 1921, now draws 1,200 exhibiting artists and fills every motel room from Albuquerque to Taos with eager buyers. Taos painter R. C. Gorman's *The Navajo Woman* is one of the most familiar icons of twentieth century American art, a notoriety that does not bother Gorman. "*The Navajo Woman*," he told an interviewer in 1994, "has bought me my cars, my home, and my dinners in Venice. Venice, Italy, by the way." The late Santa Fe sculptor Allan Houser, a Chiricahua Apache, revived the art of monumental stone statuary in America with his spare, fluid, powerful human figures. What he once said about his work is an affirmation that a good many Indian artists would share: "I work not just for myself, but to honor the American Indian. I hope to draw attention to centuries-old Indian values, especially concepts of living in harmony with nature that can benefit all people, if only given the chance."

■ BUYING POTTERY

Psst!—want a bargain on some prehistoric Southwestern pottery?

No, you don't. If the price sounds too good to be true, it is. Chances are that it either was obtained illegally, or it's a fake.

The U.S. Archaeological Resources Protection Act of 1979 outlawed the removal of Indian artifacts from all federal lands, and most states, including New Mexico, have similar laws regarding their state lands. Federal and New Mexican officials are coming down hard, and consequently most—though not all—Indian arts galleries in Santa Fe have quit dealing in them. "I'm completely out of that business," said one dealer. Added another, "The best way they have of enforcing these laws is to create a lot of paranoia out there, and they've done that." Most of the trade in artifacts has gone underground.

As for counterfeits, "There is a terrific number of them out there, and they've become so good that it's difficult to tell the difference," said another dealer. "There are some potters that can make them with the exact techniques and materials used 600 years ago."

There are potfuls of money to be made in bogus or illegal ceramics. Legitimate Mimbres or Anasazi vessels start at about $2,500 and climb toward the stratosphere—say about $25,000.

Advice for the amateur collector? Beware of "bargain" prices. Buy from a reputable gallery or collector, and make certain the seller will take it back if it later proves to be a fake. Insist on documentation certifying where and when the pot was recovered—the best proof would be that it was in a private or museum collection before 1979.

Or maybe best of all, just go ahead and buy a fake—a signed one, sold legitimately as a reproduction. The price will be palatable, and you'll never lose any sleep over it.

Interested in pottery of contemporary design? The most important guideline is also the simplest: buy what you like. Ignore its potential investment value; that's a crap shoot.

Run your finger along the inside of the pot. If it's made by the classic coil-and-scrape method it will be slightly rough and irregular, though it shouldn't be lumpy. Cast ceramics will be smoother (and much less valuable). The decorative painting or carving should be even and precise and geometrically pleasing. The architecture of the vessel is important, too; no poorly proportioned pot can be rendered elegant by the designs applied to it.

Indian pottery is a rapidly evolving art form; what you buy today may become an anthropological treasure in only a generation or two. The best pieces are worth their considerable prices.

PUEBLO POTTERY OF NEW MEXICO

Pueblo Indians have been making pottery for utilitarian use and for sale or barter for 1400 years. The practice of making them for barter declined toward the middle of the nineteenth century, when the opening of the Santa Fe Trail flooded the region with imported goods. But with the coming of the railroad in the 1880s, and the arrival of appreciative visitors, Pueblo potters realized the commercial potential of their pottery, and entered a new period of improvement and exploration. These pots from Zuñi and Laguna pueblos were made during this period.

ZUÑI POLYCHROME, 1890

Zuñi Pueblo, located south of Gallup, New Mexico, near the Arizona border, was visited by conquistador Francisco de Coronado in 1540.

Laguna Pueblo is found in central New Mexico between Albuquerque and Grants and has a long pottery tradition.

LAGUNA POLYCHROME, 1910

ZUÑI POLYCHROME FETISH, 1920

Ácoma pottery has long been valued by collectors. Hand-drawn, intricate, geometric designs, as the one below by S. Chino, are typical. Clays used by the different pueblos come from nearby sources, and Ácoma clay is noted for being especially white.

Ácoma Pueblo resides high on a mesa west of Albuquerque.

ÁCOMA POLYCHROME POT

Santa Clara Pueblo has produced many famous pottery families, among them the Gutierrez, Tafoya, and Naranjo. This pot by Anita Suazo is typical of Santa Clara carved pottery.

Santa Clara Pueblo is located on the road from Santa Fe to Taos.

ÁCOMA POT IN BLACK AND WHITE

SANTA CLARA POT
WITH BEAR CLAW DESIGN

SAN ILDEFONSO JAR, 1910

The polychrome pot above was typical of San Ildefonso Pueblo pottery until María and Julian Martínez began to make their famous black-on-black pottery designs. Their work is now world-famous, and it often commands more than $5,000 per piece. Many members of the extended Martínez family have also become exceedingly famous, and their work is invariably bought by collectors.

SAN ILDEFONSO POT,
MARIA MARTINEZ

The Jémez Pueblo pot to the left is typical of modern, sophisticated work found in galleries in Santa Fe.

Jémez Pueblo is located in the Jémez Mountains northwest of Santa Fe.

JÉMEZ POLYCHROME POT

The beautifully crafted, three-inch, black-on-red pot to the right was made by C. G. Loretto of Jémez Pueblo and recently purchased by the author of this book, Lawrence Cheek.

JÉMEZ PUEBLO POT

Figurines have long been a part of Cochiti Pueblo ceramics. Storyteller dolls, first made famous by Helen Cordero, are favorites, and cheap imitations abound. The male storyteller doll to the left was fashioned by Ada Suina, who puts coat after coat of slip on her figurines to achieve subtlety and gloss.

Below, a figurine in the shape of a turtle was made by Helen Cordero.

COCHITI PUEBLO
STORYTELLER DOLL

Cochiti Pueblo is located by Cochiti Lake, west of Santa Fe.

COCHITI TURTLE FIGURINE

■ HISPANIC ART

The Spanish settlers of New Mexico lived hard lives on a hard land, but they were not barren of artistry. New Mexico's rigors never stifled the Spanish soul.

Among the earliest artistic expressions was furniture, adzed and built by hand out of soft ponderosa pine, and decorated with chiseled designs of religious icons, fruit, vines, prancing lions, and abstract geometric figures such as rosettes. As Pueblo craftsmen were employed to build some of the furniture, Indian motifs such as chevrons, cornstalks, and ziggurats cross-pollinated the Spanish traditions for a unique New Mexican style. The hand-painted modern imitations that have formed the cornerstone of "Santa Fe Style" speak of a yearning for simpler times—and a romanticization of the Spanish Colonial era in the Southwest.

More important to the perpetuation of Spanish culture were the *santos*—small wooden statues of Roman Catholic saints that held places of honor in both home and church. The carving of *santos* in northern New Mexico is an art form that has

Furniture was one of the earliest artistic expressions of Hispanic art in New Mexico. The chest (above) was built and carved by Mexican artisans around 1840. Mexican dance masks (opposite) on display in the Museum of International Folk Art in Santa Fe.

continued in an unbroken line for more than three centuries, passed along from generation to generation.

Santa Fe merchant Rey Montez, whose father was a *santero* (sculptor of saints), explained that the art of making primitive *santos* began in New Mexico after Spain realized that the new land was not the lode of gold that had been expected, so the mother country made little effort to export its sophisticated religious art here. Because of the colony's isolation, New Mexican *santos* quickly acquired an artistic character of their own. The figures are usually elongated and almost always melancholy in expression—even today.

"We Spaniards are very fatalistic," explained Montez. "And we are not to forget the sorrow and suffering that was endured on our behalf, particularly in the images of Christ. The *santos* remind us."

Montez, who has a downtown Santa Fe gallery specializing in modern *santos*, says that all kinds of people buy them: Christians, Jews, Hispanics, Anglos. Some buy them for devotional purposes; others are collectors.

"I have an atheist who buys a *santo* every year," Montez told me. "Finally I asked him why. He said, 'It's pretty and it makes me feel peaceful.'" It seems enough to ask of a cottonwood saint.

Today, contemporary Hispanic art is flourishing in the striking multimedia work and ceramics of artists like Pedro Romero and the paintings of artists like Anita Rodriguez and Federico Vigil. Vigil's work can be seen in several of the city's museums and in the county courthouse, where he was commissioned to paint a spectacular mural.

For one weekend every July the Plaza is converted into a traditional Spanish Market. Among the hundreds of Spanish arts and crafts sold here look for *santos*, carved and painted furniture,

A santo from the Spanish Market.

weavings, and embroidery. The Contemporary Hispanic Market is held the same weekend and is located just off the Plaza on Lincoln Avenue.

■ ART MUSEUMS

Santa Fe blooms with museums devoted to crafts, historic and modern, and to fine arts. Unless otherwise noted, the museums below charge admission.

Center for Contemporary Arts of Santa Fe. A private, non-profit museum whose exhibits of visual art tend to be *very* contemporary and provocative—and sometimes just mystifying. There is also a film series and a performing arts series comprising music, dance and readings. *291 E. Barcelona Road (about one mile south of the Plaza, off Old Santa Fe Trail); (505) 982-1338.*

Tin nicho *by Bonifacio Sandoval.*

Santera *Marie C. Romero works on the preparation of one of her* santos.

Georgia O'Keeffe Museum. New Mexico's most celebrated artist finally received her due recognition in Santa Fe when this private, non-profit museum opened in the summer of 1997. Thirty-seven paintings, drawings, watercolors, and sculptures are already in its collection, with many more expected to come. ~~211~~ *Johnson Street; (505) 995-0785.* 217

Institute of American Indian Arts Museum. A division of Santa Fe's IAIA, a nationally recognized college for American Indian artists, the work here is an alternative to the more commercially appealing Indian art in the galleries. Paintings and sculpture here may be beautiful, enigmatic, ironic or bitter—or all of these at once. *108 Cathedral Place (one block east of the Plaza); (505) 988-6281.*

Museum of Fine Arts. One of the Southwest's oldest and best art museums, founded in 1917. The emphasis is on twentieth-century New Mexican art. A permanent exhibit is devoted to the works of Georgia O'Keeffe. *107 W. Palace Avenue (one block west of the Plaza); (505) 827-4468.*

(Tip: It's economical to buy a four-day pass to all five branches of the Museum of New Mexico—Museum of Fine Arts, Museum of Indian Arts and Culture, Museum of International Folk Art, and the Palace of the Governors.)

These two sculptures are from the Tesuque-Shidoni Gallery and Foundry. The one above, by John Martini, is titled Orange Bird of Biloxi. *At left is Dean Howell's work* Time Marker for Indigenous People #1.

Museum of Indian Arts and Culture. Opened in 1987, this superb museum features an enormous display of pottery from eleventh-century Anasazi to contemporary Pueblo and Navajo—and even a few Anglos working in Indian traditions. Native artisans give demonstrations in pottery, jewelry, or other arts, and docents give worthwhile tours (call for times). *710 Camino Lejo (two and a half miles southeast of the Plaza, off Old Santa Fe Trail); (505) 827-6344.*

Museum of International Folk Art. The permanent exhibit is the Girard Collection, an immense omnium-gatherum of more than 100,000 dolls, dollhouses, masks, weavings, religious icons, angels, monsters, toy trains . . . . In the museum's own words, "the collection defies categorization." Some borders on fine art, some is pure kitsch. Some visitors find it overwhelming—just too much. A Hispanic Heritage wing displays folk and religious art. *706 Camino Lejo (two and a half miles southeast of the Plaza, off Old Santa Fe Trail); (505) 827-6350.*

Wheelwright Museum of the American Indian. This private museum was founded in 1937 by Mary Cabot Wheelwright, who became friends with Hastiin Klah, a Navajo medicine man. The changing exhibits housed here feature mainly contemporary Native American artists. *704 Camino Lejo (two and a half miles southeast of the Plaza, off Old Santa Fe Trail); (505) 982-4636.*

The Museum of Fine Arts (above) is a classic example of Spanish/Pueblo Revival architecture. A display entitled Harbor Scene *(opposite) at the Museum of International Folk Art.*

■ SANTA FE OPERA

Founded in 1957, the Santa Fe Opera is an anomaly among American opera companies. It attracts an international crowd, it presents an American or world premiere every season, it performs in a theater open to the stars (and the rain), and its general director, John Crosby, is the same man who founded the company four decades ago.

When Crosby came to Santa Fe in 1956, he was a walking musical department store. He had studied half a dozen instruments, formed a dance orchestra, studied composition with Paul Hindemith, and conducting with Rudolf Thomas. In his plan for the Santa Fe Opera, he observed, "We chase our talent off to Europe to perform, when we in this country have so many beautiful places, and Santa Fe is one of the most beautiful of all." He also observed the summer rainfall at his parents' Santa Fe home in 1955 and '56 and concluded, incorrectly, that the climate was so dry that out of 18 performances over a two-week period, only two were liable to be rained out. These two summers he'd seen were abnormally dry. After four decades of soggy *Zauberflötes* and *Traviatas*, the gap in the roof is now scheduled to be closed by 1998, although the sides of the theater will still be open to the nocturnal desert air.

One of the town's most popular attractions is the opera amphitheater near Tesuque. (courtesy, Santa Fe Opera)

Every season (July and August) the Santa Fe Opera presents five operas in repertory—and not just the standard Top 40. The SFO has staged *The Confidence Man* by American George Rochberg and the resoundingly difficult, atonal *Wozzeck* by Alban Berg. Crosby's game plan each season is to produce one premiere, one Richard Strauss, one little-known historic opera, one Mozart, and one Italian opera.

The 1,889-seat theater is seven miles north of Santa Fe on US Highway 84. Tickets and hotel reservations are snatched up many months in advance.

SINGING IN SANTA FE

The Phantom of the Opera is standing on the bar not two feet from my burrito and margarita, which he nearly snags as he spreads his great black cape, bat-like, and sings:

> *The music of the night . . .*

The house lights are dark, the emotional mood intense, the singing stunning. This is no smoky nightclub; it's serious musical theater that just happens to be happening in (and on) a bar—Santa Fe's La Casa Sena Cantina. The performance ends, the singers take their bows, the Phantom—Greg Grissom—swaps his cape for an apron, and literally 30 seconds later he's serving coffee and taking dessert orders.

Everyone on the Cantina's staff both sings and serves, from the bartender to Grissom, who is also music director, restaurant manager, and cellar master. Nearly all have conservatory degrees in classical music performance or music theater, and they've learned to switch roles of waiter and singer within seconds.

"It takes a special talent," says Grissom, "to throw down two enchiladas and get up and become something. It's a matter of concentrating. I can tell within one day after hiring these kids whether they're going to make it."

Most of the "kids" are either stopping here in route, they pray, to Broadway or the Met; or have already been there and have fled for the friendlier life of Santa Fe.

Grissom's story, though, is unique.

He had a degree from the Interlochen Arts Academy, but in the 1980s he found himself keeping books for an investment firm based in Austin, Texas. They transferred him to a branch office in Taos, and he fell for New Mexico, big time. When they tried to pry him away for a job in California, he quit.

(continues)

He found another non-music job as catering director for the Santa Fe Hilton. One day in 1987 his secretary tossed a circled newspaper ad—"singers wanted"—on his desk. "You can follow your wallet or your heart," she said.

He auditioned at the Cantina, singing "On the Street Where You Live" from *My Fair Lady.* The music director hired him as a barely singing waiter. "He only let me sing once a night, and only 'On the Street Where You Live.' Finally I asked him why I couldn't sing more. He said, 'Because you're not good enough.'"

Rather than quitting in a snit, Grissom dug in. While making $2.13 an hour plus tips, he began paying $200 a week for voice lessons with a Met diva who had retired in Santa Fe. A remarkable baritone emerged from its cocoon. He learned opera and Broadway. He began singing much more than once a night, and in 1989 became manager of the cantina. Of course he still sings; he can't *not* sing.

"I had never done anything badly in my life before," he says. "I wasn't going to let music, which I love, become the first thing."

Yet for every Santa Fe success story like Grissom's, half a dozen talented musicians sell dresses, wait tables, scrape by. "Not nearly enough of them make a living as artists here, because there's not enough work. But I think the town is going to grow theatrically with the movies and commercials being made here, the expanding opera, restaurants, and clubs. If it's something you're really serious about, I think you can make it here. I *know* you can; I've done it for years."

I ask the Phantom: any regrets that he started too late for a major career on the musical stage? He grins broadly, without a trace of guile. "If somebody came to me and said, 'We have a major role on Broadway for a middle-aged bald guy, and we want you to take it,' sure I would. Meanwhile, I live in the most beautiful place in the United States and people stand in line to hear me sing."

■ ART OF ADOBE

If you do it with your family, with your children, with someone you love, the act of laying adobes, of building shelter from earth, is one of the most profound experiences you can ever have. With every course of mud mortar you lay, and every adobe brick, as the walls rise, it's like watching your children grow up.

Orlando Romero is talking about an experience that forms the architectural soul of Santa Fe, but one that only a few modern Santa Feans have experienced—building one's own house with handmade adobe bricks. The tradition is almost extinct. Romero is a dinosaur with mud on his feet.

The irony is that adobe—dirt, water, and straw, among the the least expensive of building materials ever devised—is nearly unaffordable today. Adobe is dirt cheap, but the labor to create it isn't. Fifty years ago, a Santa Fe family could invest a year's labor, evenings and weekends, to build a house, but today most people work full-time jobs and time to build a house just doesn't exist. Even wealthy folk who import their money to Santa Fe are reluctant to invest in real adobe. Robert Vigil, a Santa Fe builder, says the shell of an adobe house today costs 30 to 50 percent more than the same in wood frame and faux adobe stucco.

But adobe's romance abides.

You can begin to understand it in early morning or evening light. The old houses on Acequia Madre and Old Santa Fe Trail, made of mud bricks and bathed in mud plaster infused with wisps of straw, actually appear to glow. The low sun transmutes the mud into gold. It's tempting to believe the popular story that the sixteenth-century Spanish explorers saw an adobe pueblo basking in the evening light from a distance and assumed it was gold—hence the fabled Seven Cities of Cíbola—but the legend of Cíbola resonates far back in medieval Spain, and has nothing to do with adobe. *Que lástima,* too bad.

There are other legends about adobe that ring untrue. One is that it is an excellent insulator, hostile to modern utility companies. No, says Vigil. When he builds an adobe house, he adds a border of insulation between the bricks and the outside plaster. Another is that it lasts forever. Also not true: adobe devises numerous strategies to try to melt back into the earth. It will lick up water from the ground by capillary action and erode from inside, or wash away on the outside in a rainstorm. Earthquakes are bad news; adobe has no tolerance for lateral movement.

On the other hand, the oldest building in use in New Mexico—Santa Fe's Palace of the Governors, built in 1610—is adobe. Carefully maintained, an adobe building will weather the centuries.

New Mexico's Indians had long built with mud before the *Entrada,* puddling it up into free-form walls, but the Spanish introduced the use of adobe bricks. They had learned it centuries earlier from their own occupiers, the Moors: the word "adobe" is derived from the Arabic *al-tub,* "the brick." The technique for making and laying the brick has changed little. Mix dirt, water and straw, then pour it into wooden forms to make bricks of a standard 10 x 14 x 4 inches and let them dry in the sun. Pry them out of the forms and let them bake, or "cure," for a few more days. Then layer them into walls with mud mortar. Contemporary infidels sometimes mix asphalt into the adobe to improve its stability, but this compromises its earthen color and texture. Traditionally, mud plaster was applied to protect the exterior walls, and it used to be the women's job to replaster them once a year. Today stucco clads most of Santa Fe's modern adobe homes, reducing the maintenance burden.

Vigil grew up in an adobe house in Santa Fe, which had more than a little to do with his current occupation as a homebuilder. In 1977, he was teaching school, needed a house, and didn't have much money—so he did exactly what his family had done for generations. He made 10,000 adobe bricks by himself. He chopped 35 trees in the Jémez Mountains for *vigas*, or roof beams. Then he built the house. It was 1,100 square feet, and it cost $15,000. Romero, a historian who has written a beautiful book on adobe, did much the same thing. His 1,000-square-foot house cost him less than $10,000. "The contractors wanted $150,000," he says in amazement.

The emotional appeal of adobe architecture is easy to sense but hard to explain. Adobe enthusiasts often talk about feeling a sense of connection to the earth, that

Making adobe bricks is a craft; making them into a building, an art.

there is no sharp line where nature ends and architecture begins. Adobe has a re-assuring sense of solidity; no other kind of building offers such comforting refuge in a howling storm. And it ages gracefully, acquiring character instead of shabbiness.

But Romero says the most fundamental reward of adobe is the act of creation, fashioning shelter out of the earth itself. "Maybe I'm speaking like a poet here, but you should do it with someone you love," he says. "It's like a monumental childbirth."

MUD HOUSES

In the winter of 1884–85, an enterprising journalist named Charles Lummis walked from Cincinnati to Los Angeles, sending dispatches to the Los Angeles Times *along the way. Unlike many other Anglos of his century, he was enchanted by the ancient capital's architecture and lifestyle.*

Around the four sides of the plaza are most of the leading business houses—some in rather handsome blocks—and outside these lies the residence portion of the city. These New Mexican dwellings look odd enough to Eastern Eyes. Nearly all are adobe, and a majority only one story high, though there are some three-storied adobes. But don't let yourself be fooled by nincompoop correspondents who write back home about "mud houses." These adobes are made of baked dirt, it is true, but so is your Ross County [Ohio] Bank Block. The sole difference is that you roast your clay with a fire, and these people let the sun do their brick-burning. An adobe out here knocks the socks—pardon my territorial elegance of diction—off of any brick or frame building, so far as anything but looks is concerned. The thickness of the walls—from two to three feet—insures comfort all the year round, and an adobe is cool in summer and warm in winter.

These houses are not generally very gorgeous outside, but within they are as capable of decoration as any other kind of buildings. You get into one of those large, handsome rooms, 18 feet high, finely papered and furnished, carpeted with Brussels, and you will laugh at your prior conception of "mud houses." Even the ruder dwellings of the lower class are very comfortable and pleasant. It would be a good scheme if the board shacks of Eastern shantytowns could be replaced by these neat little adobes. The more pretentious houses here are built in a square, with a placita (little plaza) in the middle, and many have remarkable fine gardens besides. One

Ácoma Pueblo, circa 1880. (Museum of New Mexico)

thing strikes you as you look down upon the city—the universal flatness. Probably there are not 20 pitch roofs in the whole place, and but few mansards. A Mexican, you know, always has two stories to his house—the roof serving as floor to a sky-thatched attic as big as all outdoors.

. . . The countless burros, driven through the streets by Mexicans or Pueblos at a reckless gait of half a mile an hour, and generally loaded with wood, will look queer to you. It must be a semi-science, loading these little fellows. The wood—in crooked sticks of cedar, about two feet long—is laid in a kidney-shaped pile as big as the burro, across the pack-saddle, and held in shape by an adroitly-wound rope. I'd like to see a tenderfoot pack one of these loads—bet he couldn't make three sticks stick. So what with the people, the burros, and the queer little houses that pay no more attention to alignment than a dog does to catnip, one finds here street scenes as unlike as possible to all American ideas.

—Charles Lummis, *Letters from the Southwest,* 1885

SEEING SANTA FE

SANTA FE IS A WALKER'S CITY, and not only because it is compact and fairly flat. Those are the pedestrian reasons (forgive me). Much more importantly, Santa Fe has a visual and tactile romance that can't be fully appreciated through a car window.

An arched niche cut in an adobe wall, a vine or flower spilling color through it. An early nineteenth-century house wrapped around an all-but-hidden courtyard. A whimsical sculpture planted in a patio or vacant lot. A private shrine dedicated to St. Francis or the Virgin Mary. The ethereal auburn-to-gold glow of adobe walls in the early evening sun.

Also, the streets are narrow, the traffic befuddling, and there's hardly ever a place to park. So walking Santa Fe makes practical sense.

You can stroll at random, take a guided walking tour (look in the yellow pages under "Tours—Operators & Promoters"), buy an illustrated guidebook (the Historic Santa Fe Foundation's *Old Santa Fe Today* is thorough but arranged alphabetically instead of by routes), or guide yourself along the two walks described in this chapter. The first route snakes through four centuries around downtown; the second takes in two centuries along Acequia Madre and Canyon Road. Neither is strenuous, but if you visit the downtown museums and a few galleries, either walk may consume most of a day.

■ DOWNTOWN WALKING TOUR

Begin at **1** **the Plaza,** which dates from the founding of Santa Fe and which has been the focus of a host of momentous events in Santa Fe history. In the 1680 Pueblo Revolt an army of furious Indians camped in the Plaza and besieged more than a thousand Spanish refugees huddled in the Palace of the Governors. In 1846, Gen. Stephen Watts Kearny led his army into the Plaza, proclaimed New Mexico a United States territory, and raised the Stars and Stripes over the Palace. In 1962 the Plaza became a National Historic Landmark.

Notice the obelisk honoring heroes of the Civil War and Indian wars at the center of the Plaza. Note the inscription on the north side, which once commemorated the bravery of those who had "fallen in the various battles with savage Indians

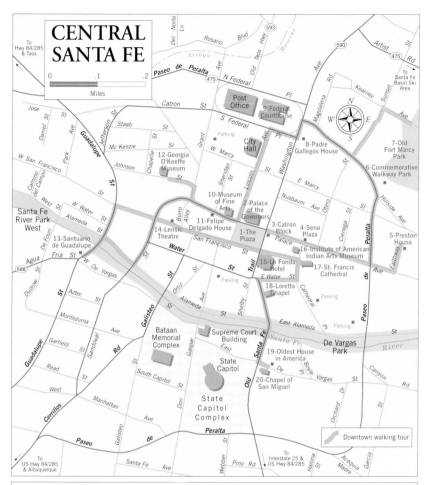

CENTRAL SANTA FE

0	.1	.2
Miles		

*Museum of Indian Arts & Culture, Museum of International Folk Art,
Wheelwright Museum, and the Center for Contemporary Arts see Greater Santa Fe Map.*

in the territory of New Mexico." The word *savage* has been chiseled out by an anonymous editor.

The grassy Plaza, shaded with lovely blue pine, American elm, spruce, cottonwood, and ornamental plum trees, remains Santa Fe's spiritual heart. Old people pass the time reading newspapers on benches, tourists stroll through in wonderment—wondering why every American city doesn't have such a gracious centerpiece—and in the evenings, when the tourist traffic begins to evaporate, teens congregate in clumps, flirting, smoking, and alternately looking cool and bored.

Ninth Cavalry Band in the plaza of Santa Fe, July 1880. (Museum of New Mexico)

The **2** **Palace of the Governors** (100 Palace Street) flanks the Plaza on the north side. Built in 1610, it is the oldest government building, aside from prehistoric *kivas*, in the United States. Like the Plaza, it has seen remarkable events in New World history. When Spanish governor Don Diego de Vargas recaptured Santa Fe from the Pueblo revolutionaries in 1693, he and his men were astounded to find that the Indians had, in essence, remodeled it into a pueblo, even converting a defensive tower on the east end into a *kiva*. Except for the 13 years of Pueblo occupation, the palace served as apartments for Spanish and then Mexican governors, and in 1862, Confederate soldiers borrowed it for their temporary headquarters. In the 1870s, Territorial Governor Lew Wallace wrote part of *Ben-Hur* while living in it.

Today, you can see the interior of the Palace, now part of the Museum of New Mexico, and get a visual sense of the world in which the early Spanish officials lived: thick adobe walls, painted white, and inside a collection of artifacts—wooden wagons or *caretas,* antique gowns, vestments, spurs, and pottery—that evoke the mood of Spanish colonial life. Some of the museum docents are from colonial Spanish families, and they relish retelling the story of the *Entrada* from the Spanish point of view.

Over the centuries the Palace has undergone much remodeling. The towers are gone, and the *portal,* a wide, covered porch that extends around the building, is a 1913 addition. Indians have been selling their jewelry and pottery in front of the Palace for hundreds of years. In recent times, vendors have been required to register with a museum program that ensures crafts are handmade by those who sell them or by their immediate families.

The main hall of the Palace of the Governors during Governor L. B. Prince's tenure in 1893. (Museum of New Mexico)

Now turn east to the corner of Washington Avenue and E. Palace Avenue and see the **3** **Catron Block,** a sophisticated Italianate Victorian building of 1891 and an example of what preservationists, in no great cheer, call "remuddling." The building's upper floor is original and beautifully preserved, but the awful (and fake) Territorial portal was tacked on in the 1960s as Santa Fe was dressing down to make itself appear more rustic and "Southwestern."

Walk a block east along E. Palace Avenue to a block-long row of contiguous adobe buildings beginning with 107 E. Palace; this includes the Arias de Quiros site and **4** **Sena Plaza.** Governor de Vargas granted Quiros, a Spanish *conquistador,* a building site here for his help in the 1693 reconquest; he planted wheat and built a two-room house, now vanished. Sena, scion of a prominent nineteenth-century Santa Fe family, later constructed the adjacent 33-room adobe mansion around a courtyard. Parts of these buildings date from the late eighteenth to the early twentieth century, but sorting them out would be impossible. Many old Santa Fe houses grew like this, by accretion over generations and centuries. The

Santa Fe Plaza in the 1880s, painted by Francis X. Grosshenney. (New Mexico Museum of Fine Arts) (left) Farolitos line the Plaza's walkways at Christmas time.

walker's treat here is Sena's shady courtyard, dominated by a mammoth cotton-wood tree and surrounded by shops. There are benches for relaxing here, along with a fountain, a biodegrading old wagon, and devil-barely-cares landscaping with vines and shrubs creeping over rough stone borders. It's the polar opposite of the primly manicured formal Victorian garden, and one of the loveliest public spaces in Santa Fe.

Continue walking east. If you're interested in books about Santa Fe or the Southwest, Palace Avenue Books, 209 E. Palace, is the specialist. Cross Paseo de Peralta, walk one more block east along Palace Avenue and then turn one block north to 106 Faithway Street to see a wild and crazy 1886 Queen Anne house—now the **5 Preston House** B&B. George Cuyler Preston was a lawyer, and his house, like the Catron Block, looks like a comfortable New England cottage.

Back to Paseo de Peralta, then three blocks curling northwest to the **6 Commemorative Walkway Park,** established in 1986. A paved path and staircase leads to the top of a hill, with 20 plaques outlining Santa Fe history along the way. Near the top is a tall white steel cross commemorating the deaths of the 21 Franciscan missionaries killed in the Pueblo Revolt of 1680. There is no memorial to the 36,000 Pueblo Indians, according to historian Marc Simmons, who died from disease, famine, and war imposed by the Spaniards.

At the hilltop is **7 Old Fort Marcy Park,** site of the first United States military post in the Southwest, begun immediately after General Kearny seized New Mexico in 1846. Nothing but mounds of dirt remain of the adobe fort, but the park is the prime place to watch sunsets over Santa Fe.

Descend from the hill, curve west (to your right) on Peralta for two long blocks, then walk south (left) on Washington Avenue to the **8 Padre Gallegos House,** 227 Washington, built around 1857. Padre José Manuel Gallegos was one of the many Spanish priests French Bishop Jean Baptiste Lamy fired after his arrival in 1851. Gallegos later married and pursued a successful career in politics. The house is remarkable for its dignity, graceful proportions, and sheer size—Padre Gallegos didn't do badly after being punted out of the priesthood.

Directly across Washington looms the 1889 **9 Federal Courthouse** at Federal Place and Lincoln Avenue, wrapped in native New Mexican granite, one of those heavyweight buildings from the time in which American courthouses were designed to convey Moral Authority through Architectural Power. Walk up the stairs to the entrance, and you're being prepped to tell the truth, so help you God. It's a mixture of Greek Revival and Romanesque style, with grand pediments and horseshoe curlicues over the third-story windows. Inside, visit the six illustrator-style landscape murals painted by Santa Fe architect and artist William Penhallow Henderson under the Federal Arts Project in 1935–37.

Continue south on Lincoln to the **10** **Museum of Fine Arts** at Lincoln Avenue and West Palace Avenue (107 W. Palace Avenue). Designed by Rapp & Rapp of Trinidad, Colorado and completed in 1917, this building shifted the Spanish Pueblo Revival style into high gear. The massive façade at the south end tries mightily to emulate the mission of San Esteban Rey at Ácoma, but its two-tone paint job and fussy decoration on the balcony spoil the effect. In New Mexico's old adobe churches, simplicity equaled nobility.

The museum's emphasis is on twentieth-century New Mexican art. On permanent display are works by Taos art colony founders Ernest Blumenschein and Bert Geer Phillips, as well as the works of New Mexico's most renowned artist, Georgia O'Keeffe.

Head west (right) on Palace to the **11** **Felipe Delgado House,** 124 W. Palace. Delgado, a prominent merchant, built this fascinating hybrid in 1890. It marries the simple adobe Territorial box to spindly Victorian woodwork—an architectural metaphor for the cultural revolution that was smoldering in Santa Fe at the time. Now a bank, the Delgado house opens to the public on the first Monday of each month.

Now take the short block west to Grant Street and head northeast (right) to Johnson Street, then west (left) to the **12** **Georgia O'Keeffe Museum** (217 Johnson Street). Established in 1997, this small museum honors one of the region's most luminous painters of the desert.

Continue west on Johnson Street, curve south (left) on Guadalupe Street, crossing the usually dry Santa Fe River, and continue half a block to the **13** **Santuario de Guadalupe,** a late eighteenth-century church that has twice endured "remuddling." Originally a typical New Mexican adobe chapel, it was dressed up as a neo-Gothic New England church in the 1880s, then recostumed yet again as a rather drab California mission in 1922. But go inside: there's a lovely and astounding baroque altar screen depicting the Virgin of Guadalupe and a Holy Trinity of three identical men. The painted screen is signed José de Alzibar, 1783.

Back north up Guadalupe to W. San Francisco Street and bear right. The three blocks from Sandoval Street to the Plaza include some of Santa Fe's most intriguing shops and galleries. There are two bookstores, including one that specializes in books and recordings from Latin America; an excellent Indian pottery gallery (Andrea Fisher Fine Pottery); and the last real people's store on the Plaza, Woolworth's. Notice the 1930 **14** **Lensic Theatre,** 211 W. San Francisco, the most exotic Spanish Colonial Revival building in town. Its cornice features a parade of creatures that look like a cross between dragons and giant sea horses—a logical Santa Fe theme.

15 **La Fonda Hotel,** which sprawls over most of a block at E. San Francisco, Shelby, and Old Santa Fe Trail, was designed in the Spanish Pueblo style by Rapp & Rapp in 1922, then enlarged and remodeled in 1928 by John Gaw Meem. Wander through the lobby and corridors to see a delightful exhibition of folk-art murals painted by Ernest Martinez, who has been the hotel's in-house artist for 40 years.

Across E. San Francisco Street at 108 Cathedral Place is the **16** **Institute of American Indian Arts Museum,** housing contemporary Indian artwork including pottery, sculpture, beadwork, basketry, and paintings. As a curator's plaque in one of the museum's exhibits notes: "An attempt has been made to stay away from the stereotypical images made of the American Indian by himself or herself. What has been selected is only a sample of an undercurrent of work that most often has been

The Lensic Theatre is an exuberant example of Spanish Colonial Revival architecture.

Screen depicting the Virgin of Guadalupe in the Santuario de Guadalupe.

overlooked—overlooked because they have no feathers, no brave warriors on horseback, no romantic view of teepees or tall seductive women with hair fluttering in the wind."

17 **St. Francis Cathedral** closes off the east end of San Francisco Street with an architectural thunderclap; it regards the low adobe neighborhood with the authority of a powerful medieval baron.

The cathedral was designed overseas in Auvergne by the French architect Antoine Mouly and his son Projectus. The Moulys journeyed to Santa Fe in 1870 to oversee construction. After a time Antoine lost his eyesight and Projectus took over. When lack of funds halted construction of the Cathedral, Projectus was contracted to build the Loretto Chapel. Before he could resume work on the Cathedral Projectus died, in 1879, and a new French architect, François Mallet, was employed. Then in a real-life Romanesque soap opera Mallet became entwined with the wife of Lamy's nephew, and was shot dead on San Francisco Street in 1879. The architect who finally finished the cathedral was the nephew of Joseph Priest Machebeuf—who had been in seminary with Bishop Lamy in France and come with him to the United States. The younger Machebeuf revised and finished the building, which was consecrated in 1886. It is an excellent French cathedral, convincing in every respect except for its perfunctory pipe organ and the odd, painted *reredos* depicting guitar-playing American saints.

Around the corner on Old Santa Fe Trail is Bishop Lamy's other architectural monument, **18** **Loretto Chapel.** This was the chapel of the Loretto nuns, the most famous of whom was Lamy's lovely young niece, Marie, who left France with her uncle when she was a child. She was educated by the Ursulines in New Orleans, then, barely in her teens, she traveled to Santa Fe in

(above) Marie Lamy, niece of the famous Bishop Lamy. (courtesy of Loretto Motherhouse Archives) (opposite) The "miraculous" staircase of Loretto Chapel.

1857, along with her best friend from the convent. Marie entered the Loretto novitiate, becoming Sister Francesca. Legend has it that she played the piano beautifully, and when her own brother came to Santa Fe and became a priest under Lamy's tutelage, she always tried to have a new piano piece ready to play for him when he came to visit.

Design and construction of the Loretto Chapel were undertaken by Projectus Mouly, the 18-year-old son of Antoine Mouly, architect of the Cathedral, who was going blind and was unable to help his son with the work. When his work was criticized, he resigned, took up drinking among "bad company," and died of pneumonia.

Finished in 1878, the chapel's light, graceful Gothic Revival design forms a pinprick of conscience in the city's skyline as opposed to the moralist thunder of the cathedral. Now deconsecrated and privately owned, there is a small admission fee to see inside.

A well-worn legend, impossible to verify, swirls around the graceful spiral staircase to the choir loft. Somehow the chapel was completed without one, and there was no room to retrofit it. Ladders wouldn't do, because the chapel was built to serve a girls' school, and modesty was a concern. The Sisters of Loretto decided to dedicate a novena (devotional) to St. Joseph, patron saint of carpenters. On the ninth and last day of the novena, a man with a toolbox appeared on a donkey and built the "miraculous staircase," which has no central support—it's a rigid wooden spring, a miracle indeed of nineteenth-century engineering. When the staircase was finished, the sisters looked for the carpenter to offer payment. He had vanished. Some versions of the legend maintain that the miraculous carpenter was St. Joseph himself.

This walking tour ends along De Vargas Street, across the Santa Fe River in the **Barrio de Analco**, which after the Plaza is Santa Fe's oldest neighborhood. It was first occupied by Tlaxcalan Indians from Mexico who accompanied the earliest conquistadors and missionaries as servants, then resettled by soldiers after the 1693 reconquest. Several of the private homes on alley-like De Vargas Street date from the eighteenth century. Note especially the many turquoise doors and shutters on this street, an old New Mexico tradition now in revival. Hispanic folklore reveres the color for its ability to ward off evil—the Devil, some believe, cannot pass through a turquoise door. Equally magical is the color's pure radiance in contrast with an adobe wall, especially in low amber sunlight. Time your visit to De Vargas Street for early evening, just before sunset.

"The oldest inhabited house in the United States," from Harper's Weekly *in 1879.*
(Museum of New Mexico)

The **19** **"Oldest House in America"** at 215 E. De Vargas allegedly incorporates part of a puddled-adobe pueblo dating from about A.D. 1250, but its *vigas* have been dendrochronologically dated from 1740 to 1767. There is an admission charge, and it's scarcely worth seeing.

Across the street at 401 Old Santa Fe Trail, the **20** **Chapel of San Miguel** was built around 1626 and destroyed at the start of the Pueblo Revolt. The present structure, rebuilt in 1710 and much modified over the years, holds an intriguing carved and painted folk-churrigueresque *reredos* installed in 1798. When the chapel was last restored in 1955, excavators found shards of Anasazi pottery under the floor.

■ ACEQUIA MADRE/CANYON ROAD WALKING TOUR

With about 80 galleries flanking historic Canyon Road, this two-mile walking tour could take days—and eat your credit card alive, depending on your artistic

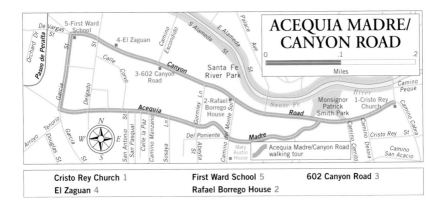

Cristo Rey Church 1	First Ward School 5	602 Canyon Road 3
El Zaguan 4	Rafael Borrego House 2	

resistance. But walking Canyon Road is definitely the way to see it; it's the equivalent of a vast art museum of extraordinary variety and vitality, and you wouldn't drive through an art museum. For people unable to walk the full length of the road, there is a pay lot in the 800 block across from El Farol and very limited street parking.

When walking along Acequia Madre, use caution: the street is narrow and there is no sidewalk. When returning down Canyon Road, pop into as many galleries as time permits. Usually only two or three pieces are visible through the windows, and they may not be representative of the surprises inside.

Begin at Garcia Street and Acequia Madre. Acequia Madre translates as "mother ditch," which is exactly what this is: constructed in the early 1600s to irrigate the fields south of the chapel of San Miguel, the Acequia Madre served as the southern border for the Santa Fe settlement up until the Pueblo Revolt. Today it forms a linear moat separating the houses on the south from the street, and at certain times of the year, notably autumn, it has a lovely, brook-like air, shaded by yellowing elm trees. Each spring—for over 380 years—Acequia Madre residents have joined together to weed and clean the ditch.

Many of the homes along Acequia Madre date from the mid- to late nineteenth century, and this is one of the best streets in Santa Fe to note their quirks and textures and handmade details. Note the miniature footbridge, sculpted adobe wall and gate with wrought-iron lanterns at 506 Acequia Madre, a perfect union of architecture and folk art impossible to imagine anywhere but in Santa Fe; note too the unusual adobe archway over the fence at 937 Acequia Madre. Recall the great architect Louis Kahn's declaration that the brick said, "I like an arch." Well, adobe brick doesn't much like an arch, but it can be tricked into forming one—until it melts back into the earth, which is what adobe likes.

Acequia Madre joins Canyon Road at the 1000 block. Continue up Canyon Road and veer right to visit **1 Cristo Rey Church.** Designed by architect John Gaw Meem, the prime proponent of Santa Fe's Spanish Pueblo Revival style, it was built in 1940 primarily with labor by parishioners. It is said to be one of the largest twentieth-century adobe buildings on earth. The parishioners, mostly Hispanic, worked five days a week for wages of $2 a day supplied by the archidiocese, and then they donated their labor on Saturdays. They laid 180,000 heavy adobe bricks, but as one parishioner, Alfonso "Trompo" Trujillo, recalled later, "Just as hard as we were working it seemed like it wasn't even working."

I thought it overbearing on a first visit, but later came to appreciate it. Meem indeed evoked the *spirit* of New Mexico's eighteenth-century Spanish churches here, allowing pure sculptural form to become architecture. The two massive towers express immense strength, but unlike St. Francis Cathedral they embrace earth rather than sky. Inside is a monumental high baroque carved stone *reredos,* transplanted from the long-ago demolished military chapel of La Castrense on San

El Zaguán on Canyon Road has been called one of the architectual treasures of New Mexico.

Francisco Street. It dates from 1760. The front doors of Cristo Rey are usually locked, but visitors may enter through the second door on the south *portal.*

Backtrack to Acequia Madre, then take the Canyon Road fork to the right. In Spanish times, this was *el camino del cañon,* a road used to ferry firewood by burro from the mountains east of town. Most of the houses along the road date from the eighteenth and nineteenth centuries, and have been pressed into service as restaurants, studios, and galleries today. A few still serve as private homes.

The **2** **Rafael Borrego House**, 724 Canyon Road, is a classic Spanish adobe with a Territorial *portal* grafted on; the original building dates from the mid-eighteenth century. Geronimo, a classy restaurant, currently resides within.

The nameless house at **3** **602 Canyon Road** now is home to an art gallery, and is well worth a visit inside to experience the radiant color, texture, and emotional warmth of mud-plastered interior walls. Few Santa Feans do this any more because of the cost and sweat involved, but see how the brilliant sunlight streams through the windows here to counterpoint the much more gently luminous accompaniment of the earth-straw walls. The building was begun around 1760, and rooms were added until about 1900.

4 El Zaguán (pronounced "El Zah-WAHN), 545 Canyon Road, is cited in *Old Santa Fe Today* as "one of the architectural treasures of New Mexico." No argument here. In afternoon winter light its 300-foot-long dusky pink façade, punctuated by turquoise shutters, radiates a glow that can best be described as ethereal. It dates from 1849, and serves today as private apartments. Pioneer archaeologist Adolph Bandelier lived here around 1890, and he designed the public garden at the building's west end, which is maintained by the Historic Santa Fe Foundation.

The **5** **First Ward School**, 400 Canyon Road, is one of those wonderful buildings that drives architectural historians to drink: it can't be filed in any neat stylistic slot. Built in 1906, it looks as though one architect had drawn a properly dignified neoclassical building, then while he was doing lunch, a prankster colleague came along and added a Queen Anne witch's hat instead of a pediment. Most recently the school housed a contemporary art gallery with all-white walls, so the only historic character left is on the outside.

At least a dozen Canyon Road galleries display large-scale sculptures out front or in courtyards, another compelling reason for walking. The northern New Mexico light, particularly in fall or winter, creates striking effects upon whatever it falls. This surely helps sell the art, but keep in mind: it won't glow like this on the back porch in Michigan.

PHOTOGRAPHING SANTA FE

The amateur photographer stepping out in Santa Fe, camera around neck, may in the first flush of euphoria believe that he or she has been delivered to the Promised Land. The heavenly light, constellation of cultures, tawny colors, and ancient architecture are seductive indeed. But the only promise here is that you'll have to work to get memorable pictures. Santa Fe and its environs are more difficult to photograph than many more prosaic places.

Your first problem is contrast. The New Mexico sun frequently creates too much of it—highlights too brightly lit, shadows too deep. The answer is to shoot in the early morning or late evening light, or pray for a day when high humidity or wispy clouds soften the sun. Photographer Eduardo Fuss, who shot most of the photos for this book, prefers evening light. It is warmer, because dust kicked into the air during the day filters the light toward the red edge of the spectrum. Mornings offer the advantage of calmer air, so foreground foliage doesn't dance around.

A second problem is the ghosts of thousands of professional photographers who've been here before you. It may seem daunting to come up with a fresh image of Santa Fe or Taos, something that hasn't already been done better on a postcard. Advice: focus on details. A weathered blue window frame on an adobe house, rather than the whole house. A footbridge over the Acequia Madre, encrusted in orange autumn leaves. Shooting the sunset over Santa Fe from Fort Marcy Park is a compelling temptation, but the details tell Santa Fe's story more eloquently.

Indians present a special problem for the photographer. "The moment you raise your camera to your eye, they will turn away, or turn their heads down," says Eduardo Fuss. The reasons are obvious, from their point of view: they don't want to be exploited, nor viewed as exotic objects. Solution: either shoot unobtrusively or ask permission (and perhaps offer a small modeling fee).

Above all, look *intently* at photo opportunities, imagining what the sunlight might do to scenes at different times of day or in a different season. And be patient. I made the traditional pilgrimage to the San Francisco de Asís church in Ranchos de Taos one evening, and was thoroughly depressed to find a dozen amateur and professional photographers jockeying for position around the church's hind end, immortalized by painters as great as O'Keeffe and photographers as untouchable as Ansel Adams. When the last light seemed to fold into the eastern clouds, the clot of photographers dissolved. I hung around, just in case. New Mexico's light is as fickle as the lottery. And I won: right at sunset, the clouds broke and the church's crosses rose in silhouette in a pinkened sky.

In northern New Mexico, the right photo is always worth the wait.

T O W N O F T A O S

I AM DRIVING INTO TAOS at the sorcerer's hour. The sun has set at my back over low Carson Mesa, leaving a thin crepuscular strip of pink and yellow light evaporating into the night sky above. Ahead, Taos's lights are blinking on in the valley, huddled feebly below 11,819-foot Taos Mountain. Above the great rock, October's full moon is rising, forcing its way through silvered wisps of clouds. Sorcery, indeed. Love at last light.

Taos, as well as its surrounding countryside and nearby pueblo, have been bewitching otherwise sensible people into writing paragraphs like that for more than a hundred years.

Mabel Dodge Luhan, the New York sophisticate who came to Taos in 1917, first saw the place at about the same time of day I did, and eventually wrote the classic *Edge of Taos Desert*:

> Looking at this definite, sudden, precise earth-form that towered there so still [the mountain], I saw something again that I had never noticed in nature. It seemed to me the mountain was alive, awake, and breathing. That it had its own consciousness. That it knew things. . . . The mountain seemed to smile and breathe forth an infinitely peaceful, benevolent blessing as the light faded away from it.

Author John Nichols, who arrived in 1969, wrote in a modern classic, *If Mountains Die*:

> My eyes, and the eyes of all Taoseños, are forever attracted to the mountain. Nobody can travel the valley without centering off its bold presence. It is the central symbol in our lives to which the eye is always drawn. Some of us may take it for granted, yet in our subconscious it breathes heavily, an exclusively solid shape in the otherwise ever-changing, sometimes ugly, often beautiful, and too often unfortunate landscape through which we travel.

I reach Taos and bunk down for the night in an old but pleasant motel about a quarter-mile from the house where Kit Carson resided from 1843 to 1868. My room has cable TV and a New Mexican beehive fireplace. I build a fire in the requisite beehive manner—make a teepee out of three or four split pine logs—and

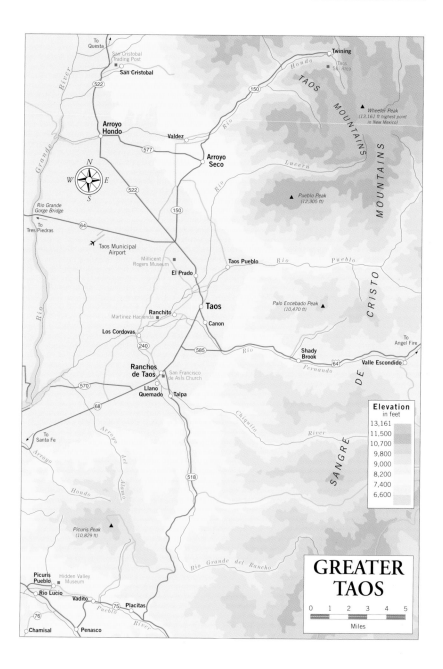

GREATER TAOS

To Questa

San Cristobal Trading Post
San Cristobal

Twining
Taos Ski Area

Hondo

TAOS MOUNTAINS

522

▲ Wheeler Peak
(13,161 ft highest point
in New Mexico)

Arroyo Hondo

Valdez

577

Arroyo Seco

Rio

Lucern

522

▲ Pueblo Peak
(12,305 ft)

Rio Grande Gorge Bridge

150

To Tres Piedras

64

✈ Taos Municipal Airport

Millicent Rogers Museum ■

El Prado

Taos Pueblo

Rio   *Pueblo*

SANGRE DE CRISTO MOUNTAINS

Taos

Ranchito

Martinez Hacienda ■

Canon

▲ Palo Encebado Peak
(10,470 ft)

Los Cordovas

240

585

Rio

Shady Brook

64

Valle Escondido

To Angel Fire

Ranchos de Taos

San Francisco de Asis Church ■

Fernando

Llano Quemado

Talpa

570

68

Chiquito

River

To Santa Fe

Arroyo del Alamo

Arroyo

518

Hondo

▲ Picuris Peak
(10,829 ft)

Elevation
in feet

| 13,161 |
| 11,500 |
| 10,700 |
| 9,800 |
| 9,000 |
| 8,200 |
| 7,400 |
| 6,600 |

Rio Grande del Rancho

Picuris Pueblo
Hidden Valley Museum ■

Rio Lucio

Vadito   Placitas

75

76

Chamisal   Penasco

Pueblo   *River*

0 1 2 3 4 5
Miles

River   *Grande*

N
W   E
S

switch on CNN for news of the real world, and wonder whether any more inspirational place than the town of Taos, New Mexico, has ever been created.

The late Taos mayor Phil Lovato, in a particularly metaphysical moment, once said, "Taos is not a city, Taos is not a town, Taos is not even a place. Taos is a state of mind and a power center of the universe."

❖

In the morning, clear of head, I decide to drive back south out Highway 68 to where I saw the moonrise, and return to Taos in daylight.

It's different, predictably. Taos Mountain is no less of a magisterial presence, but there are now roadside distractions—a blend of low-grade commercial squalor leavened by classic Taos funk and high kitsch.

First stop is an arresting teepee display. These are real teepees, as real as possible when manufactured by Anglos and sold in a place far distant from the plains, where teepees were used. The Pueblo Indians never dreamed of living in such things. The woman at the counter says they sell for $750 to $6,000, depending on size. "We sell a lot of them."

"What do people do with them?"

"Well, they live in them. Or use them for guest quarters."

Down the road, an old International Harvester truck lies abandoned and overgrown in roadside weeds. In this dry country it takes eons for things to rust away. A legend is painted on it: SPECIAL KNOWLEDGE OF THE DIVINE MYSTERIES COMING 1989—AZTEC—MAYA.

Mobile homes, adrift in an unzoned desert (a Taos city official later laments to me that Taos County has no zoning ordinance). A London Fog Factory Outlet. A Kwik Kar Wash. A boutique that sells "Jewelry-Weaving-Skulls-Furs." There is indeed a display of 20 cow skulls for sale, complete with horns.

A settlement called **Ranchos de Taos**, four miles south of the center of town, provides the entrée to Taos's allure. There is a cordon of quaint galleries here, but the real attraction is the mission church of San Francisco de Asís, which presents its back end to NM Highway 68. This is actually fortuitous, because the hand-sculpted, adobe-buttressed back of this modest church is one of the purest architectural forms in North America. Its totally blank, brown adobe walls and uneven geometry drink in the sun as it glides across the sky, integrating the Spanish concept of *sol y sombra* (sunlight and shadow) into the architecture. As G. E. Kidder Smith wrote in *The Architecture of the United States,* "one almost shakes in its presence."

LETTERS FROM GEORGIA O'KEEFFE

Dear Mabel [Dodge Luhan]—

It is 5 a.m. — I have been up for about an hour — watching the moon grow pale — and the dawn come — I walked around in the wet grass by the Pink House — one bright — bright star — so bright that it seems like a tear in its eye — The flowers are so lovely — I came over here to the Studio — so I could see the mountain line — so clear cut where the sun will come — . . . .

—Georgia

My best greetings to you Henry McBride— . . . .

I have the most beautiful adobe studio — never had such a nice place all to myself — Out the very large window to a rich green alfalfa field — then the sage brush and beyond — a most perfect mountain — it makes me feel like flying — and I don't care what becomes of Art —

We wired Marin to come out — and he came — He is having a great time too — Stieglitz says we are being ruined for home — and I feel like saying I am glad of it —

When you say you like Mabel — I must tell you — you really dont even imagine half of what you are liking — Just the life she keeps going around her would be a great deal — but that along with this country is almost too much for anyone to have in this life — However I am standing it well — never felt better — I often think how much it would all entertain you — Do write me that you are having a good summer — and if you are not — just get up and leave it — and go where you will have a good time — or like something or other — Have I painted? I dont know — I hope to — but I really dont care

There are four nice careful paintings — and two — Others —

No — there are five careful ones. . . .

—Georgia O'Keeffe, summer 1929

Georgia O'Keeffe in Taos, 1929.
(Museum of New Mexico)

Georgia O'Keeffe reduced the church to near abstraction by stripping away everything but light and form. "I had to paint it," she wrote. "The back of it several times, the front once. I finally painted a part of the back thinking that with that piece of the back I said all I needed to say about the church."

People say that this is the most photographed and painted building in New Mexico, a claim impossible to verify, but we do know that this little church moved Ansel Adams to take up his rather successful career in photography. In 1930, Adams and Paul Strand were both staying in Taos with their mutual friend Mabel Dodge Luhan. Adams noticed that whenever something interesting seemed to be happening in the sky, Strand would toss his camera in the car and dash down to Ranchos de Taos to photograph the church. Adams was so impressed with Strand's photos that he gave up his plan of being a concert pianist and dedicated his life to photography.

The church of San Francisco de Asís in Ranchos de Taos. (photograph by Lawrence W. Cheek)

Kitchen in Kit Carson's house, where the frontiersman and his wife, Josefa, ate meals with their many children.

■ EARLY TAOS

Taos is a corruption of the Tewa Indian words "tua-tah," meaning "red willow place." Its Spanish presence is even older than Santa Fe's, with the pioneer explorer Juan de Oñate having appointed a priest, Francisco Zamora, to the mission at Taos Pueblo in 1598. By 1615, a number of Spanish farmers were staking out the valley in the lee of the haunting mountain.

Taos began to assume an important economic role in New Mexico in the 1700s with its annual trade fair, a convergence of convenience in which Puebloans, Comanches, Utes, Apaches, and eventually Spaniards and Americans would all suspend their usual hostilities for a month and meet to trade furs, food, whiskey, and other goods. This was possible only because of Taos's isolation 70 miles north of the capital, where the Spanish governor would have enforced the Spanish crown's ban on commerce with "foreigners."

By the early 1800s, Anglos were settling in Taos in significant numbers, the most famous of whom was Christopher "Kit" Carson. He was a fascinating contradiction of a man—a noted killer of Apache warriors who spoke several Indian languages and eventually adopted an Apache orphan, among numerous other foster children. An 1860 newspaper profile described him as a man with "an

Kit Carson in 1850.

in-fy-nite small chance of legs [who] sits upon a horse like a king. I have never seen a man presenting a more regal aspect than this veteran mountaineer, when mounted upon his favorite steed, and dashing along like the wind." He married a Taoseña, Josefa Jaramillo, described by a contemporary as having "beauty of the haughty, heart-breaking kind—such as would lead a man with a glance of the eye, to risk his life for one smile." Carson lived with her in a rambling, 12-room house (now the Kit Carson Museum) just east of the Plaza from 1843 to 1868, when he died of an aneurysm.

The most famous (and notorious) event in nineteenth-century Taos was the Revolt of 1847, a bloody footnote to the quiet American seizure of New Mexico the year before. A few months after Gen. Stephen W. Kearny had claimed the territory for the United States, a core of Mexican loyalists in Taos, allied with some Pueblo Indians, revolted, storming the governor's house and killing him with arrows as his wife and children and Kit Carson's wife, Josefa, desperately tried to cut a hole through the back wall of the house and escape. The revolutionaries then scalped the governor and, after tacking his scalp to a board, paraded it around the Taos Plaza. The revolt lasted less than three weeks, and Indians suffered the severest losses—more than 150 dead in a final, decisive battle at Taos Pueblo on February 3. When the rebel leaders were tried at Taos before a judge whose own son been killed in the revolt, their accusers included the three Mexican women who'd been in the house with Governor Bent, the governor's wife, a Mrs. Boggs, and Mrs. Kit Carson.

■ AMERICAN ARTISTS DISCOVER TAOS

The "discovery" of Taos by artists and intellectuals beginning around 1900 was no fluke, but a reaction to what those people saw as the dehumanizing effects of industrialization, overcrowded cities, and conflict in Europe and the Eastern United States. Taos, in its simplicity and great natural beauty—even given the hardships of its isolation—appeared to be a desert Nirvana. D. H. Lawrence wrote:

> There is something savage, unbreakable in the spirit of the place out here—the Indians drumming and yelling at our camp-fire at evening . . .
> I am glad to be out here in the south-west of America—there is the pristine something, unbroken, unbreakable . . . . It [is] good to be alone and responsible. But also it is very *hard* living up against these savage Rockies.

Between 1898 and 1942 Taos became a mecca for disaffected artists, writers, and intellectuals seeking a new spiritual landing. Two academically trained New York artists, Ernest Blumenschein and Bert Phillips, were the accidental pioneers. On a sketching trip from Mexico to Colorado, their wagon broke down near Taos in 1898 and they decided to stay. Over the next 40 years an astonishing variety of artists followed—impressionists, expressionists, assorted modernists, and traditional "Western" painters. The attractions aren't hard to discern: the dramatic New Mexico light, the Spanish and Pueblo cultures, and the magnificent physical environment. It was an environment, that for many artists, tended to place human beings in appropriate perspective. Artist John Marin wrote from Taos that New Mexico was a land of "Big Sun heat. Big storm. Big everything—a leaving out of that thing called man." Good description.

Ernest Blumenschein in his Taos studio.

During this time, Taos's most influential celebrity was a New York socialite—the term may not be adequate—named Mabel Dodge, who arrived in Taos in 1917. Wrote historian Roxana Robinson, "Mabel was a rich and frequently married woman from Buffalo who collected people and created situations." Shortly after her arrival in Taos, she created many astounding situations, divorcing her husband, marrying a Taos Indian, Tony Luhan, and gathering a coterie of artists from D. H. Lawrence to Georgia O'Keeffe.

O'Keeffe didn't stay long in Taos, but she was stunned by New Mexico's high desert sunlight and what it did to the organic material it fell upon. "Its dryness reduced plant and animal life to essential forms, suggestive of the way Georgia instinctively simplified her images," wrote Laurie Lisle in *Portrait of an Artist*. O'Keeffe bought a ranch in Abiquiu, 50 miles southwest of Taos. She created abstractions out of reality—the reality of animal skulls and blooming flowers she

Ernest Blumenschein captures the magic of New Mexico light in his painting Sangre de Cristo Mountains. *(Anschutz Collection, Denver)*

discovered right around her home—and both mesmerized and pissed off the American art establishment. In the early 1940s, when someone suggested to the director of the Museum of New Mexico that Georgia O'Keeffe was becoming a pretty important artist, and it might be appropriate to commission her to paint a mural for Santa Fe's St. Francis Auditorium, he reportedly replied that he didn't want some "so-called woman artist's bone-littered landscape on the walls."

POWERFUL PEOPLE

*T*hrough the months while [D. H.] Lawrence and Frieda hesitated about coming to Taos, I willed him to come. Before I went to sleep at night, I drew myself all in to the core of my being where there is a live, plangent force lying passive—waiting for direction. Becoming entirely that, moving with it, speaking with it, I leaped through space, joining myself to the central core of Lawrence, where he was in India, in Australia. Not really speaking to him, but *being* my wish, I became that action that brought him across the sea.

"Come, Lawrence! Come to Taos!" became in me, Lawrence in Taos. This is not prayer, but command. Only those who have exercised it know its danger.

❖

Lawrence hurried over to our house in the morning ready to begin our work together. As I never dressed early in the morning, but took a sun-bath on the long, flat, dirt roof outside my bedroom, I called to him to come up there. I didn't think to dress for him. I had on moccasins, even if my legs were bare; and I had a voluminous, soft, white cashmere thing like a burnous. He hurried through my bedroom, averting his eyes from the un-made bed as though it were a repulsive sight, though it was not so at all. My room was all white and blue, with whitewashed walls, sunny, bright, and fresh—and there was no dark or equivocal atmosphere in it, or in my blue blankets, or in the white chest of drawers or the little blue chairs. But Lawrence, just passing through it, turned it into a brothel. Yes, he did: that's how powerful he was.

❖

In that hour, then, we became more intimate, psychically, than I had ever been with anyone else before. It was complete, stark approximation of spiritual union, a seeing of each other in a luminous vision of reality. And how Lawrence could see! I won't try to tell you what we said, Jeffers, because I can't remember.

—Mabel Dodge Luhan, *Lorenzo in Taos,* 1932

■ GROWTH AND THE ART MARKET

"I was at the Hog Farm—one of the original communes—for a party last night," laughs Taos author John Nichols. "I've never seen so many old hippies in my life. I would bet you half to two-thirds of them are in real estate today."

Historic Taos is dying, as Nichols sees it. Short version: the hippies swarmed in during the 1960s, eventually became middle-class, made money, and soon land values were escalating.

Says Taos Mayor Fred Peralta, whose family stretches several generations into Taos's past, "Lately, the last seven or eight years, a lot of people have been coming in and buying retirement homes. These are people with substantial money, who don't need to depend on the local economy. We have lots of home offices, people connecting to their businesses with a PC and a modem."

There are few jobs in Taos except in the tourist industry, which pays dismal wages. Consequence: children of families that have lived around Taos for 300 years are moving, typically to Albuquerque, which enjoys a real-world economy.

But Taos's astounding natural attributes continue to make it an artists' community. There are about 80 galleries in town, some 250 working artists, and the Taos Institute of Arts, which comprises classes in everything from Navajo weaving to magazine writing.

"My dad came here as an artist in 1903," says Ouray Meyers, himself an artist and gallery owner, born here in 1938. "I think there's a magic here that either attracts or repels people. We say the mountain either accepts you or it doesn't. It's intangible; a feeling that you belong or you don't. Obviously, I belong. Frederick Remington came here and couldn't do anything, and ended up disliking Taos."

Meyers thinks some of the changes that Nichols and Peralta regret have been good for Taos. "It makes life easier for an artist, because a lot of art collectors come here, and that puts a lot of us in a position where we can make a living. But we also lose some of our ambiance in the process."

Visitors to Taos will notice some differences between the galleries here and in Santa Fe. The middle-class collector looking for a nice piece of work for $250 or $1,000 may score better in Taos; the collector in search of something on the cutting edge—and probably more expensive—will find more in Santa Fe. "Taos is a great place to produce art," says Ursula Bell, director of the Taos Institute of Arts. "But the best art that's produced here isn't sold here—it goes to New York, Los Angeles, and Europe."

(preceding pages) A winter sunset illuminates the peaks of the Sangre de Cristo Mountains.

PART OF THE EARTH

Millicent Rogers (1902–1953) was the granddaughter of one of the founders of the Standard Oil Company. She enjoyed a cultured upbringing in the East and was for a time a fashion model and designer. In the last six years of her life, she discovered Taos, moved here, and endowed a fine museum dedicated to Native American arts. Describing her life in Taos to her son, she wrote:

I felt that I was part of the Earth . . .
  I felt the Sun on my surface and the Rain
I felt the Stars and the growth of the Moon

Under me Rivers ran

And against me were the tides

The waters of rain sank into me

I thought if I stretched out my hands

They would be earth and green
would grow from them

And I knew that there was no reason to be lonely

That one was everything

—Millicent Rogers, *letter,* circa 1950

■ VISITING TAOS

The town of Taos, four miles north of Ranchos de Taos and two miles south of Taos Pueblo, is an enjoyable place to wander on foot, taking in the galleries, small cafes, and the laid-back ambiance.

Even in the dark of winter Taos can be filled with light. Brilliantly sunlit white snow blankets the rugged peaks of the Sangre de Cristos, forming a spectacular stage set. Stark cottonwood trees guard icy rivulets running through the town.

During the Christmas season, as in Santa Fe, thousands of *farolitos* illuminate the Plaza and nearly every building in town

Tiny Taos is actually *congested*, thanks to the fact that US 64 and NM 68 meet in the middle of town, a block from the Plaza. Everyone should stop where the two highways intersect and take a look at the wonderful mural of a *santero* (carver of saints) painted by local artist George Chacón on the side of a building in 1989. Bristling with symbolism, the anonymous *santero* is carving sculptures representing the Mexican-American family, the individual with a positive outlook, and the struggling single parent. But his *santos* look eerily like ghosts.

This heart of town looks as though it is trapped in a time warp between the eighteenth century and the impending twenty-first. As in Santa Fe, the old, brown adobe buildings are mostly protected and preserved (though nothing in Taos has the temerity to rise more than two stories); the enormous, stately cottonwoods lining the main roads seem to have been there at the dawn of time—and yet, the buzz of commerce permeates everything. Taos seems to have been *invented* for tourism. There are nine art and historical museums, the world-class Taos Ski Valley (maximum 4,800 skiers per day), and more boutiques (one specializes in wine and garlic) than seem possible in a town of 4,500.

Mural by George Chacón.

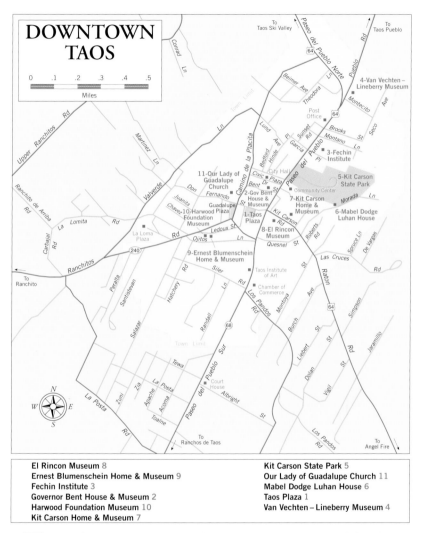

DOWNTOWN
TAOS

0   .1   .2   .3   .4   .5
Miles

El Rincon Museum 8
Ernest Blumenschein Home & Museum 9
Fechin Institute 3
Governor Bent House & Museum 2
Harwood Foundation Museum 10
Kit Carson Home & Museum 7

Kit Carson State Park 5
Our Lady of Guadalupe Church 11
Mabel Dodge Luhan House 6
Taos Plaza 1
Van Vechten – Lineberry Museum 4

1 **Taos Plaza**, located just west of the highway intersection and founded in 1790, has a modest charm, even if it was remodeled mainly in brick in 1976. The shops clustered around the Plaza tilt more toward curio than art, especially T-shirt shops. One historic curio is the D. H. Lawrence *art* collection in the cluttered manager's office of La Fonda Hotel on the Plaza's south side. Lawrence lived in

Taos in 1922–23 and 1925. He produced these 10 paintings later. The cops seized them from a London exhibition in 1929. They're hardly lewd by modern-day standards—a few rather vague butts and breasts peek out—but they do demonstrate that Lawrence was a more gifted writer than painter. A small fee paid at the check-in desk gains admission to the exhibit.

■ SITES NEAR TAOS PLAZA

There are enough historic homes and museums in Taos to keep any visitor occupied for a full day. They are listed below more or less clockwise around **1** the Plaza, beginning with the Governor Bent House and Museum. (See Downtown Taos map.)

2 **Governor Bent House and Museum.** Charles Bent, a prominent trader along the Old Santa Fe Trail and the first U.S. governor of the territory, lived here until he was scalped in January 1847. The museum displays frontier memorabilia and period furnishings. *One block north of the Plaza at 117-A Bent Street; (505) 758-2376*

3 **Fechin Institute.** Expatriate Russian artist Nicolai Fechin lived in and remodeled this two-story adobe house from 1927 to 1933, investing it with his own distinctive Russian-style furniture, doors, windows, corbels, and beams. The non-profit institute also offers more than a dozen five-day workshops in painting, drawing, and sculpture for students at all levels. *227 Paseo del Pueblo Norte, a few blocks north of the Plaza; (505) 758-1710*

4 **Kit Carson State Park.** A lovely park in the middle of town. Kit Carson is buried in the small graveyard beside his wife and nearby several other Carson namesakes. Mabel Dodge Luhan is also buried in the same graveyard. *Paseo del Pueblo Norte, between Garcia Place and Civic Plaza Drive*

5 **Mabel Dodge Luhan House.** Today a bed-and-breakfast, Mabel Dodge's three-story hacienda was once the gathering place for writers and artists including Georgia O'Keeffe, Willa Cather, Carl Jung, and Aldous Huxley. Years later actor Dennis Hopper lived in the house while filming *Easy Rider. 242 Morada Lane; (505) 751-9686*

6 **Kit Carson Home and Museum.** Carson bought this 1825 adobe house, now in downtown Taos, in 1843 as a wedding gift for his 14-year-old bride, Josefa Jaramillo. The courtyard house holds hundreds of artifacts—guns, furniture, dresses, and contemporary newspaper profiles of Carson. *One-half block east of the Plaza on Kit Carson Road; 758-0505*

7 **El Rincon Museum.** A small, family-owned museum adjacent to El Rincon Bed-and-Breakfast and Gift Shop. Native American and Spanish Colonial artifacts are on exhibit here as are Kit Carson's leather pants. *114 Kit Carson Road; (505) 758-9188*

8 **Ernest Blumenschein Home and Museum.** In 1912, artist Ernest Blumenschein became one of the six co-founders of the Taos Society of Artists. This rambling house exhibits the Blumenscheins' collection of Japanese and American Indian art as well as their own work. *222 Ledoux Street; (505) 758-0505*

9 **Harwood Foundation Museum.** Operated by the University of New Mexico, this art museum features a permanent exhibit of paintings, drawings, prints, photographs, and sculpture dating from the earliest (1910s) years of Taos as an art colony. The paintings and photographs testify eloquently to the reasons so many artists have congregated here: the power of the land and the irresistible images of its people: e.g., a painting of Taos Mountain, brooding in a winter storm as a funeral procession struggles through the snow beneath it. *238 Ledoux Street; (505) 758-9826*

10 **Chapel of Our Lady of Guadalupe.** A lovely adobe chapel built in the 1970s. A large, brilliantly colored portrait of the patron saint adorns a wall inside the chapel. *404 San Felipe Street NW, Patio Escondido.*

11 **Van Vechten–Lineberry Taos Art Museum.** This large and ambitious private museum features the work of Taos artist Duane Van Vechten, who died in 1977. Virtually unknown because she chose not to sell her paintings, she was a gifted artist who mastered many different styles. Other Taos and New Mexico artists are on exhibit as well; the museum's taste is conservative. *501 N. Pueblo Road; (505) 758-2690*

■ G R E A T E R   T A O S   S I T E S   (see the Greater Taos map on page 121)

Millicent Rogers Museum. This private museum, founded in 1956, maintains a stunning collection of Pueblo and Navajo jewelry, textiles, and pottery. Centerpiece: the Martínez Room, which showcases the development of the pottery of María Martínez and her family of San Ildefonso Pueblo. *Millicent Rogers Museum Road, 4 miles north of the Plaza on NM 64; (505) 758-2462*

Martinez Hacienda. An exactingly restored Spanish *hacienda* dating from 1804—1827, originally belonging to Don Antonio Severino Martinez, the *alcalde* (mayor) of Taos. The fortress-like 21-room adobe house is built around two courtyards with few exterior openings, testifying to the danger of Apache attacks. There are several interesting displays of Spanish Colonial furniture and implements, such as an *artesa,* a wooden bowl resembling a shallow crib, used for making cheese. *Ranchitos Road (NM 240), 2 miles south of Taos Plaza; (505) 758-1000*

■ TAOS PUEBLO

Located two miles north of town on US 64, and described more fully on page 157 in the "EIGHT NORTHERN PUEBLOS" chapter, Taos Pueblo is one of the most famous architectural monuments in the United States. Begun about the year 1200, it has been continuously inhabited by Taoseños for nearly 800 years. The tribal councils allows visitors, and there are some small shops in the pueblo. This is a quiet, traditional village, and outsiders should act with discretion.

The living room of the Fechin Institute (above). Detail of corbels which protrude from the side of a building and are the ends of the crossbeams that support the ceiling (opposite).

EIGHT NORTHERN PUEBLOS

A POTTERY EXPERT IN SANTA FE warns me that I won't save any money driving to the pueblos and shopping for art there, as opposed to the galleries in Santa Fe and Taos.

He's wrong.

On a pleasantly cool spring morning I walk through a creaky screen door into a modest adobe house in Santa Clara Pueblo, about 30 miles north of Santa Fe. Like many of the buildings in the pueblos, it is both home and shop. Perhaps a hundred bowls and vases are showcased on a series of handbuilt shelves. One immediately captures my attention. It's a small black-on-red Jémez bowl, only three inches high, decorated with ancient symbols for feathers, clouds, and lightning, and it is perfect. The price is $75.

The proprietor and I have a conversation, too. He invites me to Santa Clara's August 12 feast day—a day of celebratory dancing and eating on which non-Indian strangers are frequently invited into Indian homes to share the festive food—and he volunteers a sober opinion about the prime issue among New Mexico's Pueblo tribes at the moment.

"We [Santa Clara] voted not to go into gambling," he says. "It brings in bad blood. And yes, it hurts the artists. Somebody spends $75 at the Pojoaque pueblo slot machines, that's $75 they don't have to spend for our art."

The numerous Pueblo tribes of New Mexico are the descendants of the great Anasazi, Mogollon, Sinagua, Salado, and Hohokam migration that took place from about A.D. 1150 to 1450. These people, speaking different languages and coming from different cultural traditions, eventually proved able to live in harmony.

When the renowned Swiss psychiatrist C. G. Jung visited New Mexico in 1924–25, a Taos Pueblo chief asked him, "What are they seeking? The whites always want something; they are always uneasy and restless. We do not know what they want. We do not understand them. We think that they are mad."

Jung asked the chief why he thought that.

"They say that they think with their heads."

"Why, of course. Where do you think?"

"We think here." The Indian pointed to his heart.

Contemporary author Ron Swartley, in a book entitled *Touring the Pueblos,* sketched a not dissimilar picture of the Puebloans' character. "Through countless generations the Puebloans have learned something of the essence of life; learned what is important and what is not; resisted the temptation to become preoccupied with the frivolous concerns which mainstream Americans all too often get caught up in."

The chain of pueblos stretching from Santa Fe to Taos are banded together in a council called Eight Northern Indian Pueblos. Many visitors from Santa Fe make the one-day trek, expecting to encounter exotic culture, architecture, and art. Some, frankly, return in disappointment. It is difficult to have a conversation of any real depth with a Puebloan until you truly get to know him or her—most talk, fundamentally cordial, will be about the weather. The architecture of the villages, with the exception of Taos, consists of low-roofed homes, usually of adobe, or of HUD's dreary government-issue design, arrayed more or less at random around a large, bare-earth courtyard. Many areas are off-limits to the public.

When the railroad was completed in the Southwest during the 1880s, it brought with it settlers, tourists, and revived interest in Pueblo arts. Here, a train passes near Laguna Pueblo. (Underwood Archives, San Francisco)

However, each pueblo has a scattering of small shops, many of them in peoples' homes, selling everything from bola ties to excellent jewelry and pottery. It helps, if you're a prospective buyer, to know the subject. "My son makes all these," says a very elderly shopkeeper in Taos Pueblo, showing me a collection of strikingly contemporary necklaces of steel. Then, *sotto voce,* she adds, "you have to watch out. Some people around here get their Indian jewelry from factories."

If it were not for the arts, particularly pottery, the pueblos would be dreary and impoverished places. They mainly owe the revival of this striking art form to a remarkable San Ildefonso woman named María Martínez.

To a certain extent, each pueblo has developed a distinctive pottery style: glossy black vases for Santa Clara, undecorated micaceous ceramics for Taos. But there has been so much innovation and cross-fertilization that today it is hard to identify some pieces with any certainty. This is one instance, however, when it seems safe to say that tourists and their expectations have influenced native art for the *better.* It is no longer functional—that is, nobody buys a $1,000 San Ildefonso jug planning to pour Beaujolais from it—but the architecture, the intricacy of the painting, the imagination, and the excellence of the designs far surpass the pottery being made a century or more ago.

Indian pots and textiles have been in great demand by collectors for over a century. Kachina dolls, in this case made from a corn cob (opposite) by artist Barbara Howard, are also a much sought-after Indian art form.

❖

Early in 1995, Gov. Gary Johnson opened a giant *acequia's* floodgates for gambling on New Mexico's Indian reservations by signing a gaming compact with all the tribes. New Mexico has sanctioned horse racing for years, but Indian gaming promises to involve much more money, more tourism, more controversy, and, probably, more broken dreams.

The pueblos will be allowed to offer virtually any kind of gaming Las Vegas does, and the construction of mammoth casinos straddling US 285 and NM Highway 68 from Santa Fe to Taos seems to promise all the choices anyone could want.

All except peace and bucolic quiet, perhaps. In a February 1995 article in the *Santa Fe New Mexican,* the manager of Tesuque Pueblo's Camel Rock Gaming Center envisioned the future of the highway between Tesuque and Taos as an entertainment strip 55 miles long. Fortunately, as of the writing of this book, there are still long stretches of beautiful countryside along this route.

■ VISITING THE PUEBLOS

The pueblos north of Santa Fe are for the most part strung along a highway traversing magnificent open country—the Jémez Mountains visible to the west, the Sangre de Cristos to the north and east, and a vast, infinitely variable sky overhead. Author Willa Cather once wrote of the sky here: "Elsewhere the sky is the roof of the world; but here the earth was the floor of the sky."

Most pueblos are located off the main road. In looking for Tesuque and Taos, remember that both are near small towns of the same name, located along the highway. The pueblos are at some distance.

If possible, plan your visit for a feast day or dance day; the action will be infinitely more rewarding than wandering around an all-but-deserted plaza.

■ TESUQUE
[*Te Tsu Geh* ❖ Cottonwood Tree Place / Land of the Spotted Water]
Tesuque's original Tewa name as pronounced by its inhabitants 300 years ago meant (according to *New Mexico Place Names*) "a spotted dry place," an apt description of a creek here that disappears in the sand and periodically emerges in

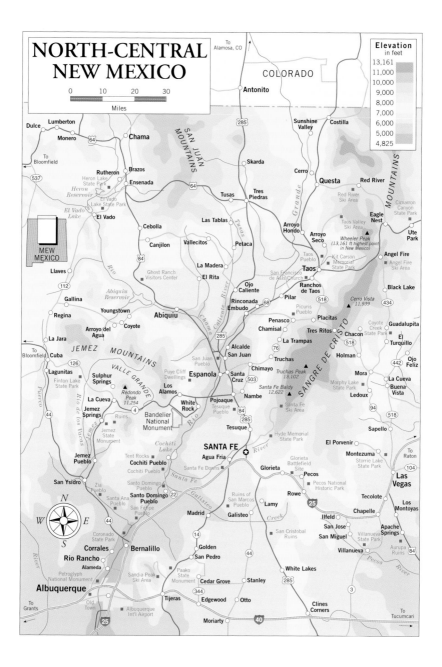

NORTH-CENTRAL NEW MEXICO

0   10   20   30

Miles

Elevation
in feet

13,161
11,000
10,000
9,000
8,000
7,000
6,000
5,000
4,825

To
Alamosa, CO

COLORADO

Antonito

MEW
MEXICO

Dulce   Lumberton
Monero   64
To
Bloomfield
537   Rutheron   Brazos
Heron Lake
State Park   Ensenada
Heron
Reservoir   El Vado
Lake State Park
El Vado
Lake   El Vado
Cebolla
Canjilon   Vallecitos
84
La Madera
Llaves   Ghost Ranch
Visitors Center   El Rita
112
Gallina   Abiquiu
Reservoir
Regina   Youngstown
Arroyo del   Coyote   Abiquiu
Agua
La Jara   JEMEZ   MOUNTAINS
To
Bloomfield   Cuba   126
Lagunitas   VALLE GRANDE
Finton Lake   Sulphur
State Park   Springs
Redondo
Peak
11,254
La Cueva   Los
Jemez   Alamos
Springs   Ruins
44   Bandelier
National
Monument
Jemez
State
Monument
Jemez   Cochiti
Pueblo   Lake
Tent Rocks
San Ysidro   Cochiti Pueblo
Zia   Cochiti Pueblo
Pueblo   Santo Domingo
Pueblo
Santa Ana   Santo Domingo
Pueblo   Pueblo   22
San Felipe
Pueblo
Madrid
Coronado
State Park
Corrales   Bernalillo
Rio Rancho
Alameda
Petroglyph   Sandia Peak   Paako
National Monument   Ski Area   State
Monument   Cedar Grove
Albuquerque
Old
Town   Tijeras   344   Edgewood
To   Albuquerque
Grants   Int'l Airport
25   Moriarty   40

Chama   SAN JUAN MOUNTAINS
285   Sunshine   Costilla
Valley
Skarda   Cerro
Questa   Red River
Tusas   Tres   Red River
Piedras   Ski Area   Cimarron
Canyon
State Park
Las Tablas   Eagle
Nest
64   Grande   Arroyo   Taos Valley
Hondo   Ski Area   Ute
Arroyo   Wheeler Peak   Park
Petaca   Seco   (13,161 ft highest point
in New Mexico)
Taos   Kit Carson   Angel Fire
Pueblo   Memorial   Angel Fire
State Park   Ski Area
San Francisco   Taos
Ojo   de Asis Church
Caliente   Ranchos   Black Lake
Rinconada   de Taos
Embudo   68   Pilar   Cerro Vista
Picuris   11,939   434
Penasco   Pueblo
Chamisal   Placitas
Tres Ritos   Coyote   Guadalupita
Alcalde   76   La Trampas   Chacon   Creek   El
San Juan   518   State Park   Turquillo
San Juan   Truchas   Holman   442   Ojo
Pueblo   Feliz
Puye Cliff   Chimayo   Truchas Peak   Mora   La Cueva
Dwellings   Espanola   13,102
Santa   503   Morphy Lake   Buena
Cruz   Santa Fe Baldy   State Park   Vista
White   Pojoaque   12,622   Ledoux
Rock   Tesuque   Nambe   518
Pueblo   84   Santa Fe   Sapello
285   Ski Area
Tesuque   Hyde Memorial   El Porvenir
State Park
Montezuma   To
SANTA FE   Stornie Lake   Raton
Agua Fria   State Park
Glorieta   104
Glorieta   Battlefield   Las
Site   Vegas
Santa Fe Downs   Pecos   Tecolote
Ruins of   Pecos National
San Marcos   Rowe   Historic Park   Chapelle   Los
Galisteo   Pueblo   Lamy   Montoyas
Galisteo   Ilfeld
Creek   San Jose   Apache
San Cristobal   San Miguel   Villanueva   Springs
Ruins   State Park
Golden   Villanueva   Aurupa
14   Ruins   84
San Pedro   44
White Lakes
285
Stanley   3
Clines
Otto   Corners   To
Tucumcari

Rio   Grande
Chama   River
Rio   Puerco
Rio de los Vacas
SANGRE DE CRISTO
Tusas   River
Santa Fe   River
Galisteo   Creek
Pecos   River

spots. Spanish settlers mispronounced the original Tewa name, and this bungled word was re-translated years later as "cottonwood tree place." In Spanish and English, Tesuque is applied to the region around the pueblo.

Tesuque's Camel Rock Casino, located along the road and not back in the village, currently offers 24-hour-a-day Las Vegas–style gambling in a building the size of a 747 hangar. The tribal-owned RV campground has restrooms, hot showers, and hookups—an interesting option for visitors looking to escape Santa Fe's stratospheric prices and lose their money in the Tesuque Casino instead. Fine views extend from this campground and include Camel Rock—which looks like its eponymous animal—and "the badlands," striated rock formations set against the backdrop of the Jémez and Sangre de Cristo Mountains.

Tesuque Pueblo is a small adobe village centered on a church, and its citizens do not encourage visitors. *Nine miles north of Santa Fe off US 285. The main village is one mile west of the highway; (505) 983-2667.*

■ P O J O A Q U E

[*P'o Suwae Geh* ❖ Place to Drink Water]

Thanks to smallpox imported by the Spanish, most of Pojoaque's original inhabitants died, and those who were left moved away. A ghost pueblo, Pojoaque was completely abandoned in the first part of this century, but you'd never know it today. Immense, dazzling signs visible for miles in each direction promise:

POJOAQUE CASINO, MILLIONS WON MONTHLY

The newly minted millionaires and Pojoaqueans may appreciate it; New Mexicans who cherish the Rio Grande Valley's scenery aren't so sure. The garish Pojoaque signs look like they're straight out of Vegas.

More is to come. Former ghost pueblo Pojoaque has opened a 40,000-square-foot "Cities of Gold" casino with a 1,000-square-foot bingo hall, video game hall, motel, and golf course. The tribe's population, incidentally, is now about 250. Of all the pueblos, Pojoaque most assiduously welcomes visitors. On the highway they've built a visitors' center, a small museum, and a small tribal restaurant. *Fifteen miles north of Santa Fe off US 285; (505) 455-2278.*

PUEBLO ETIQUETTE

Each pueblo in the Santa Fe–Taos region celebrates an annual feast day, a remarkable tradition that includes ceremonial dancing to the accompaniment of drums, rattles, and bells, and feasting. Although each of these celebrations honors the Catholic saint for whom the *conquistadores* named the village, ancient indigenous seasonal ceremonies and rites underlie these festivities. Tribe members will frequently invite non-Indian visitors into their homes to share the food, although this practice may be endangered because of its expense to the Pueblo families and the occasional boorishness of the guests. Some ceremonial events are closed to visitors. Call in advance; the best single source for information is the Eight Northern Indian Pueblos Council, (505) 852-4625. An annual visitors' guide to the Eight Northern Indian Pueblos is also available free at the Santa Fe Convention and Visitors' Bureau.

There are several rules of etiquette for visiting the pueblos, some of which may be culturally foreign to non-Indian visitors. These apply not only to feast days, but at all times.

- Rules on photographing pueblo buildings or ceremonies vary. Before you snap, ask at the pueblo governor's office or visitor center. Some, such as Taos Pueblo, levy a fee. Never photograph an individual or private property without asking permission.

- Don't talk or walk around during dances or other ceremonies, don't applaud, and don't ask for an explanation of the ceremony. Vernon Lujan of Taos Pueblo told the *Santa Fe New Mexican* that sometimes he responds to requests for explanations by saying, "If I tell you, I'll have to kill you." He's only kidding—but it gets their attention. Most Puebloans simply ignore the requests.

- On feast days, don't ask to come into a home for a meal, but graciously accept the invitation if one is offered. The Official Visitors' Guide to the Eight Northern Pueblos adds: "Thank your host, but a payment or tip is not appropriate."

- Never enter a pueblo *kiva* or graveyard.

- Never bring pets, firearms, alcohol, or illegal drugs into a pueblo.

- Finally, call before traveling to a pueblo to make certain it's open. Some ceremonial days are closed to outsiders.

FEAST DAYS AND DANCES

Call ahead to verify dates and for precise directions. Also consult maps as the pueblos can be tricky to find.

Ácoma.
Feast day: September 2. Sixty miles west of Albuquerque off I-40. (505) 470-4967

Nambé.
Feast day: October 4; Nambe Falls Celebration, July 4. North and east of Santa Fe off NM 503; (505) 455-2036

Picurís (aka San Lorenzo).
Feast day: August 10; dances in February; sunset dance in August. Northeast of Española off NM 75; (505) 587-2519

Pojoaque.
Feast day: December 12. Fifteen miles of Santa Fe off US 285; (505) 455-2278

San Ildefonso.
Feast day: January 23. Corn dance in June. North and west of Santa Fe on NM 502; (505) 455-2273

San Juan.
Feast day: June 24. Deer dance in February. Footraces and arts and crafts show in July. Just north of Española on NM 68; (505) 852-4400

Santa Clara.
Feast day: August 12. Various dances in February and June. Just west of Española off NM 30; (505) 753-7326

Taos.
Feast Day: September 30.
Los Comanches dance, February; footraces in May, corn dance in June. Two miles north of town of Taos; (505) 758-9593

Tesuque.
November 12. Corn dance in June and July. Ten miles north of Santa Fe on US 285; (505) 983-2667

Festivities at Santa Clara Pueblo (opposite), and San Ildefonso Pueblo (above) are colorful events that may be viewed by visitors.

■ N A M B É

[*Nambé* ❖ Mound of Earth in the Corner]

Located east of the highway, this tiny pueblo of around 600 members has perhaps the most beautiful setting of any along this route, snuggling in a green, level valley with panoramic vistas of the Sangre de Cristos. First inhabited about A.D. 1300, it contained about 200 structures when the Spanish arrived. About ten percent of these buildings remain.

In the mountains behind Nambé, Nambé Falls and Lake provide excellent opportunities for fishing, sightseeing, or hiking. Because of the elevation, the site is closed from November to March. An especially colorful day to visit the park would be the Fourth of July, when the Nambé Waterfall Ceremonial takes place at the foot of the falls.

From Santa Fe take US 285 north 15 miles, turn east on NM 503 and continue three miles to the sign at Nambé Falls, then two miles north to the entrance; (800) 94-NAMBE or (505) 455-7708.

■ S A N   I L D E F O N S O   P U E B L O

[*Po Woh Ge Oweenge* ❖ Where Water Cuts Down Through]

With its fine tradition of pottery, San Ildefonso Pueblo is an excellent place to explore the art—the population is only about 500, but most of the pueblo's families are involved in it. Black-on-black—a shiny background contrasted with a matte-black finish—remains the most popular style. Many people here are descendants of New Mexico's most famous potter, María Martínez, and her husband Julian. Both were producing pottery in the traditional polychrome style of San Ildefonso before Julian in 1918 developed his famous matte black-on-black. Because María and Julian began signing their pieces early, and at a time when this was not common, their remarkable career can be traced by collectors.

María's sisters also worked in pottery—Maximiliana, Desideria, and Juanita, as well as Clara, the youngest, who did most of the polishing. Santana and Adam Martínez, Maria Poveka, and Juanita's daughter, Carmelita Dunlap, were also important in the history of San Ildefonso pottery.

The small San Ildefonso Pueblo Museum sits next to the mission church (rebuilt in 1968). Most buildings in this village are new or reconstructed. To the north of the village lies the natural tabletop fortress of Black Mesa, where in 1694 Pueblo Indians attempted to defend themselves against the Spanish reconquest.

From Santa Fe take US 285 north 15 miles, turn west at NM 502. Continue six miles to the entrance; (505) 455-3549.

■ S A N T A   C L A R A   P U E B L O
[*Kha P'o* ❖ Spring Water]
This pueblo is also known for its pottery, in particular that of the Gutierrez and Tafoya families. As Margaret and Luther Gutierrez have recounted their family's history, pottery-making was passed down through generations, from their great-great-grandfather, Ta-Key-Sane, who made kitchen utensils for everyday use, and their great-grandfather, who added colors and began making pottery in different sizes. When Margaret's and Luther's father, Van, was young, his grandfather would take him into the hills to hunt game and to look for different colored clays, flowers, and roots for paints that would turn into different colors when they were fired. Van and his wife, Lela, were famous for their impressed bear paw designs on black, polished pots, and polychrome pots with geometric designs.

The Tafoya family's black carved bowls, polished inside and out, have an almost contemporary appeal.

The most compelling attraction here is the nearby Puye Cliff Dwellings, reached by a paved road about 11 miles west of Española. (Also see "DAY TRIPS FROM SANTA FE.") Those more engaged by nature than archaeology can continue on beyond the cliff dwellings into the Santa Clara Canyon, a lovely recreation area with four lakes, a stream, and canopies of pine, spruce, and aspen. The canyon offers 86 campsites and several cabins. *From Santa Fe take US 285 north to Española. At the second turnoff head west across the Rio Grande, then at NM 30 travel west 1.3 miles; (505) 753-7326.*

■ S A N   J U A N   P U E B L O
[*Ohkay* ❖ We Are Brothers]
Elements of about 100 homes dating from A.D. 1200 still stand here. In olden times the pueblo practiced dry farming, growing melon, cotton, and corn east of the village.

San Juan Pueblo was actually Spanish New Mexico's first capital, established by Juan de Oñate in 1598, and named by him San Juan de Los Caballeros (Gentlemen). To their later chagrin, the San Juans gave the Spaniards a warm welcome—one of Oñate's friars, according to historian Marc Simmons, "remarked that they were the best infidel people he had ever seen." They certainly were patient. It wasn't until 82 years later that the San Juan medicine man, Popé, led the Pueblo Revolt that drove the Spaniards out of the country.

One curiosity claimed by none of the other pueblos: a New England Gothic-style church, built in 1899 to replace a crumbling adobe church. Today, the pueblo operates an enormous gaming facility on the highway that offers bingo, black jack, poker, and slot machines. The village itself is off the road. *From Santa Fe take US 285 to Española. Continue north along NM 68, and turn west on State Road 74. The entrance is one mile past the San Juan Pueblo sign; (505) 852-4431.*

■ PICURÍS
[*Picurí* ❖ Those Who Paint]
Once one of the largest pueblos in northern New Mexico, with a six-story building rivaling Taos and a population of more than 3,000 people. Today only about 250 people live in the rather isolated town. The Picurís Pueblo Museum sketches

The Koshare clowns at San Juan Pueblo in 1935. (Museum of New Mexico)

(opposite) Classic Puebloan ladder at Picurís Pueblo.

A triptych of Indian artisans at work. A Navajo weaver (top, left), a Zuñi jeweler drilling holes in beads (top, right), and a Zuñi potter creating a vase using the traditional coil and scrape method (above). (Underwood Archives, San Francisco)

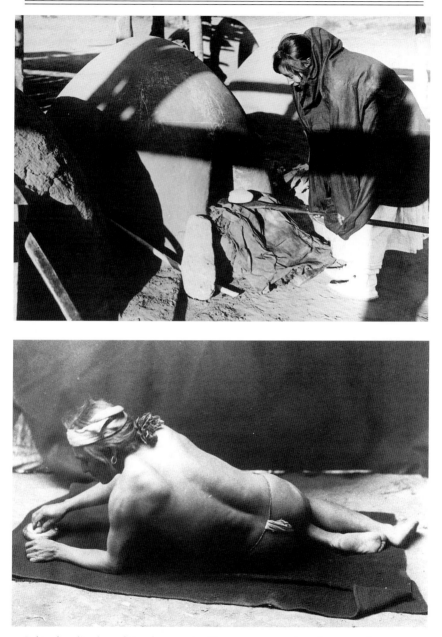

Baking bread in the traditional manner is still as common a practice today among the Puebloans as it was when this photo was taken 60 years ago (top). Indian grinding medicine (above). (Underwood Archives, San Francisco)

the village's history. Recent archaeological excavations at the pueblo unearthed several *kivas* and storage units over 700 years old.

Like the Taoseños, the people of Picurís make sparkling micaceous pottery. They also own and operate Hotel Santa Fe in Santa Fe. *From Santa Fe take US 285 north 41 miles (17 miles northeast of Española) to junction with NM 75. Turn right and continue 13 miles; (505) 587-2519.*

■ TAOS
[*Tua Tah* ✤ Red Willow Place]

Taos Pueblo is the northernmost pueblo, the most famous in literature and art, and architecturally the most ambitious. "It is the extraordinary cellular living and storage units at Taos which most excite the visitor," wrote G. E. Kidder Smith in *The Architecture of the United States.* "The piling of cube on cube coalescing with the splendor of abstract geometry to produce a scale buildup that echoes the hills." More poetically, the architectural historian Vincent Scully wrote that ". . . its syncopated masses clearly dance before the mountain's face. They are active themselves. At the same time, seen from the west, North House rises straight into the sky, and the step-backs of its south face shape the typical Pueblo sky-altar, abstracting the

Taos Pueblo (above). Deer dance at San Juan Pueblo (opposite).

shapes of the clouds. The building is once again the god of sky and mountain alike, no less wholly embodied in it than at Teotihuacán."

It is impossible to know whether this is prattle or something close to the true symbolic meaning of Taos Pueblo's astounding architecture. Pueblo life, society, architecture, art, ceremony, and spirituality are so tightly intertwined that—well, the best explanation I have seen is: "Outsiders will never get it."

Whatever Taos Pueblo *means* (if anything), it is an awesome achievement by any human standards. The pueblo probably first arose in the 1300s, but what we see today—contrary to popular legend—mostly dates from a reconstruction following the Pueblo Revolt of 1680. This hardly matters. The idea of constructing a five-story apartment building out of mud and straw and maintaining it for several hundred years has to stand as a landmark in any architectural notebook.

Those visiting the pueblo after the first snowfall of the season may see men wrapped in blankets standing at the edge of the buildings, chanting in celebration of the event.

The Taoseños don't live in their ancestral home any more—no electricity, water, or phones—but are scattered around in modern houses on their reservation. The pueblo is divided into north and south villages. Walk around the edges of the plaza between them, rather than across it—which is not considered polite. Most of the ground-floor apartments have metamorphosed into shops, and a legion of *hornos*—outdoor adobe beehive fireplaces—have sprouted around them to produce hot bread for the tourists. Taos Pueblo is not an Indian Disneyland, but it does have that potential—and, it seems to me, that temptation. *Two miles north of the town of Taos off NM 68; (505) 758-9593.*

DAY TRIPS FROM SANTA FE

THE ROADSIDE STAND WAS A RIOT OF COLOR—crimson *ristras* of dried chiles, some woven into wreaths; green and orange gourds, bushel baskets of green and red apples, drapes of ornamental corn in red, white, black, yellow. I was curious about the sign, Sopyn's Fruit Stand, in the settlement of Rinconada between Santa Fe and Taos on NM 68. This is near the heart of Spanish Colonial New Mexico, and the name on the stand hardly sounded Hispanic.

"I'm Ukrainian," answered the proprietor, Anna Sopyn, a compact woman with swirling white hair, gold-capped teeth, a face wizened and bronzed by long days in the New Mexico sun. She held out her hands, proudly. Thick, strong fingers, two of them sporting bandages. "See, I working all the time."

She escaped from the USSR in 1942, at the height of what the Soviets call the Great Patriotic War. She landed in New Mexico in 1950 and has not budged since. She tried farming, then eventually opened this roadside stand featuring apples and her ornamental arrangements of chiles and corn. We talked for half an hour, partly in her still-fractured English, partly in my nearly defunct Russian. She said she has had a good life in New Mexico. She did not miss or cherish her homeland. "They don't eat, they have nothing." She paused and smiled. "America is very good."

❖

Gospazha Sopyn is one reason why you should plan on spending more than two or three scant days in Santa Fe just cruising only the museums and galleries and restaurants. Using the capital city as a base, the center of a 130-mile circle, you can enjoy taking at least a week's worth of fascinating day trips around northern New Mexico. They include awesome mountain scenery, spooky canyons, prehistoric ruins, modern pueblos, art galleries that tend to be less expensive and less predictable than Santa Fe's, and perhaps best of all, roadside encounters with people like Anna Sopyn. Something about northern New Mexico nourishes creativity, encourages people to reinvent themselves—and they always seem willing to talk about their lives.

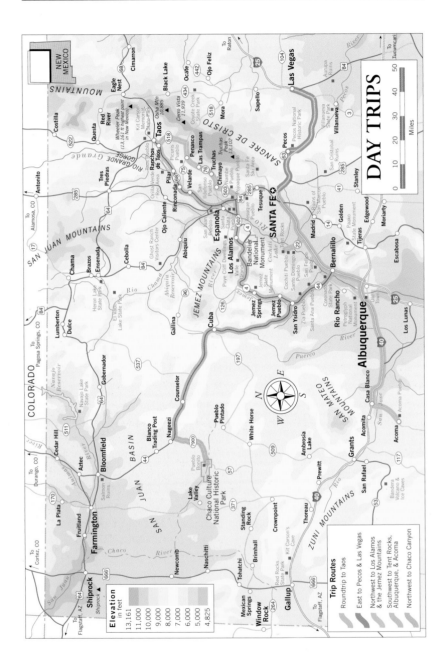

DAY TRIPS

Miles

0 10 20 30 40 50

Trip Routes

Roundtrip to Taos

East to Pecos & Las Vegas

Northwest to Los Alamos
& the Jemez Mountains

Southwest to Tent Rocks,
Albuquerque, & Acoma

Northwest to Chaco Canyon

Elevation
in feet

13,161
11,000
10,000
9,000
8,000
7,000
6,000
5,000
4,825

I recommend five discovery trips from Santa Fe:
① North along the main roads (US 285 and NM 68) to Taos and back along the "high road" through Truchas and Chimayó;
② East to Pecos and Las Vegas;
③ Northwest to Los Alamos and the Jémez Mountains;
④ Southwest to Tent Rocks, Albuquerque, and Ácoma; and
⑤ Northwest to Chaco Canyon.

All can be made as day trips except the loop to Taos, which deserves an overnight or two en route. Chaco Canyon is a *long* day trip.

Everywhere you should invest in some conversation in order to begin to understand the culture of this land, which seems to welcome anyone and any enterprise —the potters of Ácoma, the eighth-generation weavers of Chimayó, the animal-bone monger near Velarde, the nude bathers at Spence Hot Springs. Anything, it seems, can and does happen in northern New Mexico.

Anna Sopyn poses outside her fruit stand near Rinconada; one of the many roadside stands worth visiting along the highways of northern New Mexico. (photo by Lawrence W. Cheek)

■ ROADS TO TAOS AND BACK

It must be something in the piñon-scented air: New Mexico's most intriguing people and enterprises have congregated along the two routes linking Santa Fe and Taos. They have been doing so for more than 300 years.

This used to be the farm and ranch country of New Spain. An ancient New Mexican hymn describes the intimate relationship of these people and their land:

> *De la tierra fui formado,*
> *La tierra me da de comer;*
> *La tierra me a sustenado*
> *Y al fin yo tierra ha de ser.*

> (From the earth I was made,
> And the earth shall feed me,
> The earth has sustained me,
> And in the end I shall be earth also.)

The quicker route on US 285 and NM 68 mostly parallels the Rio Grande. The so-called High Road comprising NM highways 518 and 76 winds through the scenic passes of the Carson National Forest and visits several delightful little towns, including Las Trampas, Truchas, and Chimayó. Recommendation: do both. Take the Rio Grande route towards Taos and return via the High Road.

For the first 10 miles north of Santa Fe, US 285 is a four-lane highway that winds and climbs through a wide valley between the Jémez and Sangre de Cristo ranges. The hilly piñon–juniper forests thicken; wealthy Santa Feans' exurban homes peek discreetly—though sometimes flagrantly—out of the low forest canopy. You pass the famous Santa Fe Opera, almost invisible on the west side, and its neighbor, which may be the world's ritziest swap meet. Soon afterward come the booming casinos and roadside businesses both enchanting and strange.

The **Tesuque Village Market**, right off US 285 at the Tesuque exit, is a good place to stock up on day-trip provisions—the market consists of a deli, wine shop, bakery, sundry store, and cafe. It's also where saavy locals go to savor a good cup of coffee and read the *New York Times*.

Just south of the town of Velarde is a business that probably could thrive only in northern New Mexico: **Ruben's Poco de Todo.** It's closed when I stop, but Ruben

Montoya, the proprietor, is puttering around and he cheerfully opens up for me.

Poco de todo, "a little of everything," turns out to be an omnium-gatherum of used saddles, antique wagon wheels, ladders, chile powder, and animal bones. "I sell skulls, bones—people will buy anything," the 73-year-old Montoya tells me. "I don't know why, but I make good money at it." The junk is resistible, but Montoya's jive isn't—he tells me a life story of orphanages and world travel, and I tell him I'll buy a sack of Velarde chile. "No you won't," he says. "I'll give it to you." And he does.

More miles, more characters. I continued north to Velarde and the famous **Valdez Fruit Stand.** Running a fruit stand doesn't begin to describe what Herman and Loretta Valdez do. Thirty years ago, Loretta said, she quit her secretarial job to raise her children, but began to miss contact with adult people. Herman, her husband, suggested they open a fruit stand to sell produce from their orchard. They did, and it was a success. A few years later, a line in the romantic Victorian novel *Ramona* by Helen Hunt Jackson gave her an idea: The protagonist, Alessandro, left an ear of corn or a gourd at Ramona's window to suggest a liaison. Loretta began weaving gourds, ears of ornamental corn, chiles, garlic, wild grasses, and even pine cones into astoundingly elaborate and beautiful organic sculptures. Now a large staff produces the pieces under her direction, which are shipped all over the world. They sell for $5 to $5,000.

"I don't have any training in designing," she told me. "The Man Upstairs just uses my head."

In Rinconada (across the road from Anna Sopyn's place) was another remarkable entrepreneur: Jake Harwell, proprietor of **Southwest Adirondack Furniture.** Harwell told me he came to New Mexico a dozen years back from Oklahoma because "I couldn't stand the place." His shtick is stick furniture—chairs, sofas, coffee tables, bookcases—all made of thin aspen, willow, and alder sticks gathered within a 30-mile radius of his workshop and store. It's a substantial business; he said 80 percent of his work is commissioned. Stick chairs typically go for $100 to $350.

"It's hard to figure my costs, they're so low," he told me. "It's all labor. I've been making something out of nothing for 20 years. It's what I do."

❖

Continuing north on NM 68 the road travels through the mountain-rimmed valley where by 1615 Spanish farmers were setting up haciendas. Today, this is

(following pages) A cemetery along NM Highway 68 near Embudo.

unzoned desert land, both beautiful and somewhat disconcerting in its haphazard development. At the settlement of **Ranchos de Taos**, the road passes the mission church San Francisco de Asís made famous by the paintings of Georgia O'Keeffe and the photography of Ansel Adams, among scores of others. Four miles farther lies the **town of Taos** with its funky but comfortable plaza, winding streets, and adobe homes. The **pueblo of Taos**, a few miles north of town, is one of the oldest continuously occupied buildings in North America. Begun about the year 1200 (and completely rebuilt in the late 1600s), it is in essence a five-story adobe apartment house. The town of Taos is fully described in the chapter entitled "TOWN OF TAOS" on page 120. More on Taos Pueblo can be found in "EIGHT NORTHERN PUEBLOS" on page 157.

❖

Rio Grande Gorge, northwest of Taos on US 64, makes an interesting short detour. Here the valley flatlands, tinted blue-green with stubbly sage and chamise, suddenly open into a profound, black gash 650 feet deep. The highway crosses the river on the second highest bridge in the U.S. highway system, and people with severe acrophobia may want to avoid it.

The bridge doesn't shake, however, and for those who can tolerate the elevation, there are pedestrian walkways out over the yawning gorge on both sides of the bridge. The river gliding below, its color an apparent olive drab from this height, is an arresting sight. The gorge, along with the downriver Orilla Verde Recreation Area, is a worthwhile and relatively short side trip from Taos—or, if you choose, an alternative route back to Santa Fe.

After crossing the gorge, look for telephone poles on the left just beyond milepost 242. Turn left on a good, hard-packed dirt road and follow it 11 miles into the gorge where another bridge crosses at river level. The **Orilla Verde Recreation Area** begins here with an easy two-and-half-mile hike, La Vista Verde Trail, featuring many prehistoric petroglyphs. Modern wildlife is abundant here on the gorge floor; the Bureau of Land Management reports waterfowl, beaver, cougar, ringtails, and much more.

Beyond this bridge, the gorge gradually widens into a canyon, the road paralleling the slow-moving river here lined with salt cedar. The BLM has established several picnic grounds and campsites along the river (fees must be paid at the visitors' station at Orilla Verde campground). Fishing is good, with rainbow and German brown trout the customary prizes. Swimming is not recommended. It's possible to return to Santa Fe this way. The dirt road returns to NM 68 at Pilar.

❖

Most travelers will return to Santa Fe from Taos on what's known as the "**High Road**"—more of a scenic and cultural adventure if you maintain a lazy pace to enjoy it. Due to the interweaving of roads it's best to keep a highway map on hand. Take NM 68 south of Taos to NM 518, follow signs to Las Trampas and NM 76.

My lazy pace was adrenalized by a close encounter just off NM 518 at Osha Canyon. Canyon enthusiasts, my wife and I decided to explore. A few hundred feet down the trail, near a sparkling mountain stream, we heard a vivid baritone snort and gurgle. Staring into the ponderosa forest gloom, we saw nothing, but the vocal signature of a black bear was obvious. Exploration hastily terminated.

A Carson National Forest ranger later told us that it had been a dry year, so the bears had trundled down to lower elevations in search of forage. She had not heard of any violent encounters.

❖

About 25 miles south of Taos on NM 76 is the tiny pastoral village of **Las Trampas**, founded in 1751 by a colony of 12 families from Santa Fe. There's little commerce here; the prime attraction is the church of San José de Gracia (1760–76). The beautifully restored mission has broad adobe shoulders capped with delicate wooden pyramids with crosses, almost suggesting the steeple on a New England church—in Roman Catholic duplicate. (It's open to visitors June–August.) Interesting modern *santos,* carved in juniper and aspen wood by local artists, are for sale at La Tiendita, a store facing the church across the parking lot.

At first view—from an overlook along the highway—the town of **Truchas** appears to float across a grassy valley below the snow-capped Truchas Peaks, spectacular mountains soaring up to 13,101 feet. The village was founded with a land grant in 1749 and frankly changed little until the late twentieth century, many generations of residents making a living by small-scale farming. Even today the main street of Truchas looks very much like an isolated Mexican village snoring away the centuries.

But Truchas's isolation dramatically ended in 1986 when Robert Redford brought a crew to film *The Milagro Beanfield War.* All the celebrities and commotion put the town on the map. Since then, about a dozen gift shops, galleries, and B&Bs have opened. Ray Tafoya, whose family has owned the Truchas General Store for more than 50 years, said strangers still come to see the town and ask about the movie.

"Pretty good movie, huh?" Tafoya remarked. I mumbled agreement even though I hadn't seen it. Weeks later I rented the tape. It's a *spectacularly* bad movie, with little of the humor and humanity that filled the John Nichols book on which it was based. Moreover, it shows little of Truchas—Redford & Co. built sets outside the town rather than using existing buildings.

Like most of the little towns in the orbit of Taos and Santa Fe, Truchas is in the throes of enormous cultural change. Artists fleeing Santa Fe's cost of living have settled here, as well as immigrants from around the country who are charmed by Truchas's pastoral quietude and awesome scenery. Nearly all the newcomers are Anglo; nearly all the natives are Hispanic. I talked to an aging hippie who came to Truchas 25 years ago. "I stuck it out, and I'm finally accepted as a native," she said. "But for a long time they were terrified of us. I raised two kids here, and there was a lot of hostility toward them."

Weaver Harry Cordova brooked no hostility, but he's not thrilled with the way the town is changing. "There's a downside," he said. "People move out of the city because they want to live here in the country, but then they think somehow their

Truchas rests in a verdant valley of the Sangre de Cristo Mountains.

(opposite) Harry Cordova at work on his textiles in Truchas.

quality of life has gone down, and they want to bring all the things from the city with them. Suddenly septic tanks aren't good enough, and we've got to incorporate, and all that."

The Cordovas Handweaving Workshop is one of two essential stops in Truchas. Harry and his father Alfredo Cordova produce beautiful custom-woven rugs and sell them much too cheaply. Harry is cheerful and always willing to take a few minutes away from the loom to talk about his family's work. The other is Bill Franke's **Hand Artes Gallery,** one of the most interesting and eclectic art galleries in northern New Mexico. There's furniture, folk art, fine art, religious art, Hispanic art, and provocative art, like a painting of the Virgin Mary holding a live bullet.

EURALIA VIGIL:
THE TEACHER AND HER APPLES

"When we were growing up here," says Euralia Vigil, "we would never go to dances or the movies like the other kids, because we were always working. My mother would say, 'Don't worry—when they grow up they won't know how to do anything, and you will.'"

Mother's wisdom was profound. Euralia, now 66, farms a 12-acre orchard in Chimayó, 40 miles north of Santa Fe, selling her apples, jellies, pies, and chile powder at farmers' markets in Santa Fe and Los Alamos. She also has a masters' degree in education; she taught school for 33 years. Her six surviving brothers and sisters also are or were teachers, and they know ranching or farming as well.

Their father, Severo Martínez, had three months of school. Their mother, Julianita, had none; she never even learned to read. But both were determined that their children not only would get college degrees, but would use their degrees to give future generations the education they had never had.

When Euralia was born in 1928, Chimayó was an isolated Hispanic farming community without a school, without any connections, really, to contemporary America. When Euralia started school she spoke no English, and she was not taught it in today's gentle, politically correct manner. "The teachers would hit us for speaking Spanish," she recalls. "It was a very bad way to teach."

There were 13 Martínez children, but a diphtheria epidemic took five of them. There was no doctor in Chimayó. "My father tried to take the children on the wagon to Española [10 miles away], but they wouldn't make it—they would die on the way. Two of my sisters died on the same day."

❖

From Truchas the High Road descends into the drier and warmer piñon–juniper scrub land of the Chimayó Valley. Of all the villages strung along the High Road, **Chimayó** is the most interesting. It has a venerated family of weavers that has maintained their business for eight generations; a historic and (according to believers) miraculous chapel; and a famous restaurant, Rancho de Chimayó Restaurante.

Before the Spanish town was founded around 1700, there was a Tewa-speaking pueblo in this fertile valley. According to Indian legend, there was a pool here—perhaps a hot spring—whose water or mud held healing properties.

The survivors went to a private boarding school in Albuquerque because there was no bus to ferry them back and forth to the public school in Española. There wasn't enough money for tuition, so Severo paid the school in apples. "We were poor," Euralia says, "but in a sense we were also rich, because we always had everything we needed. We had close to 100 acres, and we grew everything. Apples, corn, chile, sugar cane, wheat. We had horses, cows, pigs. We never had to buy anything. And we knew how to work! The young kids do not know how to work nowadays."

Not the kind of work that matters most to her, anyway. The old ways are evaporating. "The families give their orchards to their children, and the children just let the trees die," she says. "They get work in Los Alamos—some get good jobs at the lab, others are cooks and janitors. But they're not interested in farming."

Her love for the land is profound. "Even when I was teaching, I always had a garden. The land is life to me. It is a lot of work, but work is also life to me."

It still seems a hard life. In a good year Euralia can make $1,000 a week selling produce at the farmers' markets alone. In a bad year a late freeze kills all the apple buds and she has nothing. No sign of frustration clouds her explanation. "You just have to be patient and do it all over again."

She is a short, sturdy woman, her square-cornered face weathered and arroyoed by decades in the New Mexico sun. She wears a farmer's fashions: jeans, heavy plaid shirt, a trace of earth under her nails. The rural home she shares with her husband, Victor Vigil, is small and warm and immaculate. The living room is choked with flower-print pillows and green plants and pictures of her extended family—two daughters, two grandchildren, dozens of nieces and nephews and in-laws.

Nearly all are college graduates; most are teachers.

"It's a happy life," Euralia Vigil says, "because I know I have done my part."

The present **Santuario de Chimayó** may have inherited that very site; there are archaeologically interesting remnants about, and some historical accounts have the chapel's interior smelling of an "earthen dampness," rather than dry earth and dust.

There is more mystery swirling about the chapel's origins. On the night of Good Friday in 1810, says another legend, a Chimayó settler named Bernardo Abeyta was performing the customary penances of the Society of Penitentes when he saw a bright light shining from a hole in the ground near the Santa Cruz River. He walked over and picked up, incredibly, a crucifix of the Black Christ, similar to that in the Cathedral of Esquípulas in Guatemala—a shrine 2,000 miles away that was believed to have miraculous powers to heal the sick. As the story continues, the crucifix was taken to the church in nearby Santa Cruz, but it wouldn't stay. Twice it returned—of its own accord—to the place where it was found. Abeyta got the message: he petitioned the priest in charge of New Mexico missions for permission to build a private shrine on the site. Completed in 1816, the Santuario remained in the Abeyta family until 1929, when it was turned over to the Archdiocese of Santa Fe.

Santuario de Chimayó.

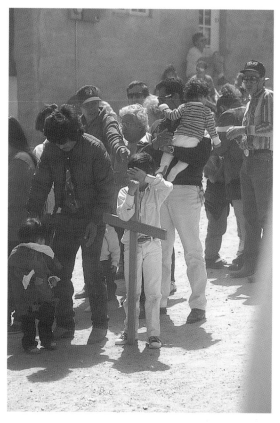

The Easter pilgrimage to Santuario de Chimayó attracts thousands of worshippers every year.

Some 300,000 people annually visit the Santuario—sometimes called "The Lourdes of America." Some come out of curiosity, some to relish its architectural beauty, and many because they believe in its curative power. During Holy Week each year, more than 10,000 believers undertake a pilgrimage to Chimayó. Some struggle to carry heavy wooden crosses.

The secular miracle of Chimayó is its chile, usually dried and ground into powder. Nowhere else in the country, nor probably in the world, does chile attain such a precise balance of fire and flavor. Several family markets in Chimayó sell bags of ground chile; one near the Santuario opportunistically markets it as "Holy chile." Holy or hellish, freeze it in an airtight container when you get home: this will help preserve the flavor.

■ EAST TO PECOS AND LAS VEGAS

The great Sangre de Cristo Mountains yield to the Great Plains on this short excursion, in the course of which we visit a national historic park and a lovely small city with a fine collection of Victorian architecture. The round trip from the city of Santa Fe is just 130 miles.

Pecos Pueblo, today a National Historical Park located on NM 63 off I-25, was founded sometime around A.D. 1300. It occupies a defensive ridge, but the site has other advantages. The Pecos River is close at hand, and the location was on the very edge of the Pueblo world, bordering the territory of the nomadic Plains Indians—which made it a crossroads for trade. Rings made by teepees set up for extended swap meets are still visible in the area.

The Pecos traders must have been nervous, however. Over time the settlement grew to have the air of a fortress, with a high perimeter wall and a five-story pueblo with no outside doors or windows. Any invader would have had to drop through a roof hatch into a darkened room, where he could reasonably expect to be greeted with a spearpoint or hatchet.

The first *conquistadores* appeared at Pecos in 1590 and were not welcomed; they decided to seize the pueblo by force. Pecos had 500 determined defenders, but it did not have rifles and cannon.

In 1598, Juan de Oñate, leader of the Spanish settlers in the area, assigned a missionary to attend to the surly Pecosans, but he had scant success in seeding the Gospel among them. In 1621 a more experienced friar, Andrés Juárez, arrived and supervised the building of a mammoth mission church, **Nuestra Señora de los Angeles.** The ruins visitors see today are not of this church, but of a smaller replacement finished in 1717. The original was destroyed, along with the priest, in the Pueblo Revolt of 1680.

After Spanish rule resumed, Pecos slid into a long, slow decline. By the 1830s, it was a ghost pueblo, victim of Comanche attacks, European-introduced diseases, and people scattering for a more hopeful life in other settlements—principally Jémez Pueblo, 80 miles to the west.

Only low walls remain of the Pecos Pueblo. One *kiva* has been reconstructed and is open to the public. The adobe shell of Fray Juárez's church still stands. Notice the arches on either side of the chancel—very rare in New Mexican missions.

❖

Las Vegas, 45 miles east of Pecos, was New Mexico's Territorial capital—for a day or so. When Gen. Stephen Watts Kearny marched into New Mexico in 1846 to claim it as a U.S. Territory, he did so from a rooftop in the little Mexican village of Las Vegas. The crowd assembled in the plaza to listen must have been perplexed, for while Kearny assured them he had come in benevolence, promising to respect their religion and property rights and protect them from Apache raids, he also added: "He who promises to be quiet, and is found in arms against me, I will hang."

When the first train steamed into Las Vegas in 1879, the village became a boom town almost overnight, attracting not only merchants and entrepreneurs but also hustlers and hoodlums. Outlaw Billy the Kid slept here—in jail—and gambler "Doc" Holliday briefly ran a dental practice before shooting a man and moving on to greater notoriety in Tombstone, Arizona. Law enforcement was so impotent that some Las Vegans eventually formed a vigilante committee, shooting suspected criminals or hanging them from a windmill in the plaza.

Civilization eventually caught up with Las Vegas—a state university opened in the 1890s—and by 1900 the prosperous town had fine Victorian homes as stately and imposing as those in Albuquerque. Mostly well maintained or restored, they offer a delightful visual treat to visitors today.

William H. Bonney, aka Billy the Kid. (Museum of New Mexico)

The Citizens' Committee for Historic Preservation has put together two self-guided walking tours, outlined in very informative free brochures available at many downtown businesses. One tour surveys the **Douglas–Sixth Street and Railroad Avenue Historic District,** which is

Downtown Las Vegas (above) features eclectic architecture as well as a comfortable Old West, small-town environment. A rainbow spans a valley in the Jémez Mountains (opposite).

mainly commercial; and the other takes in the residential **Library Park Historic District.** See especially the **Plaza Hotel,** 230 Old Town Plaza, a rambunctious three-story Italianate Victorian decorated with a curved or triangular pediment over *every* window and a grand broken pediment crowning the parapet. To the Victorian mind, excess was never wretched. The **Old City Hall of 1892,** located at 626 Sixth Street, is built in the Richardsonian Romanesque style and would look perfectly at home in Boston. Unlike Santa Fe, Las Vegas never tried to build on its Hispanic architectural heritage, but instead dressed itself in the popular styles of the East—a way of announcing that prosperity and American style had arrived in the Territorial hinterlands.

■ Los Alamos and the Jémez Mountains

"Peace is still controversial in Los Alamos," reported the *Santa Fe New Mexican* in 1994. A coalition of 41,000 children from 50 states and 53 nations had proposed a "Peace Park" at the entrance to this town, birthplace of the atomic bomb. The Los Alamos city council rejected the idea, fearing that the park would become a magnet for nuclear armaments protests.

"Couldn't you just once let them [the children] be idealistic?" an adult supporter begged the council. A foe responded: "This is the kind of peace that ultimately sees nothing as worth dying for, nothing worth going to war over. This is a peace that expresses itself in a sentimental view about human nature . . ."

The council voted no. There will be no Peace Park in Los Alamos, 35 miles northwest of Santa Fe. There is a provocative nuclear energy museum and a very rich lode of history for a town founded during, and because of, World War II. Los Alamos also leads to Bandelier National Monument and the Jémez Mountains, a long and edifying day trip from Santa Fe.

The genesis of Los Alamos was a letter from Albert Einstein to President Roosevelt in August of 1939. The physicist wrote: "It may be possible to set up a nuclear chain reaction, by which vast amounts of power and large quantities of new radium-like elements would be generated . . . extremely powerful bombs of a new type may thus be constructed." Einstein's prescient letter, along with the casing of a bomb identical to "Fat Man," which destroyed Nagasaki with vast amounts of power, is on display in the **Bradbury Science Museum** in downtown Los Alamos.

Until 1943, Los Alamos, located on a high (7,410-foot) mesa northwest of Santa Fe, consisted of nothing more than a boarding school for boys. At the midpoint of the war, the government condemned the school and created a top-secret company town to develop the bomb. The site was the third choice. Maj. John H. Dudley, who was assigned the task of finding a place for the Manhattan Project, first proposed a site in Utah, but it would have taken too much farmland out of production. Dudley then suggested Jémez Springs, 30 miles west of Los Alamos, but physicist J. Robert Oppenheimer vetoed it—Jémez Springs is in a canyon, and Oppenheimer wanted a place with expansive horizons for his team.

For the wartime families assigned to live in Los Alamos, however, the horizons were fiercely contained by security. They were forbidden even to mention the name of the town in correspondence. When babies were born, birth certificates carried a post office box number rather than "Los Alamos." There were no in-laws, no jails, no poor, no idle rich, no sidewalks. The apartments hastily thrown up for the scientists and their families frequently caught fire from their primitive coal-heating stoves—a striking irony in the nation's highest-tech town. The Los Alamos scientists referred to the weapon they were developing as "the gadget." Manhattan Project supervisor Gen. Leslie Groves referred to the scientists as "the greatest collection of crackpots ever assembled."

This series of photos captures the dawn of the atomic age at Trinity Site in New Mexico on July 16, 1945. Army photographers recorded this event, which took place following years of research by some of the world's most prominent physicists at Los Alamos National Laboratories. In the top picture you see the start of the explosion, a small cloud that seconds later rose to a height of 40,000 feet. In the next frame the explosion grows bigger and takes on the shape of an egg. The black in the middle was brighter than the sun itself according to witnesses. The third photograph shows the development of the mushroom cloud approximately five seconds after detonation. These photographs were released to the press by the army on August 17, 1945, shortly after the bombing of Hiroshima and Nagasaki. (Underwood Archives, San Francisco)

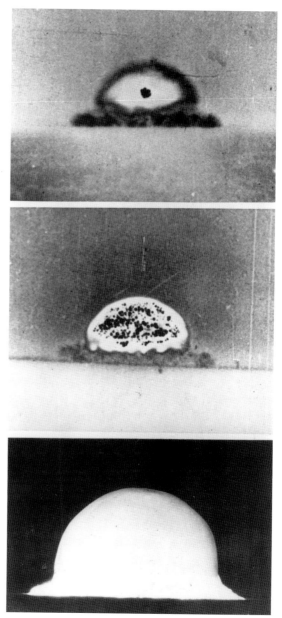

Los Alamos today remains a company town; most of its 11,500 residents work at Los Alamos National Laboratories. The lab continues nuclear weapon development, but also has branched into peacetime research in such fields as superconductivity. Controversy continues, not surprisingly. One room of the Bradbury Science Museum is dedicated to citizens' opposition, such as posters protesting "LANL's Deadly Legacy," 12 million cubic feet of buried radioactive waste.

The Science Museum is definitely worth visiting. The nearby **Los Alamos Historical Museum** covers everything from the Cenozoic Period to the Atomic Age, including an impressive display on the changing of attitudes toward nuclear power —from optimism to cynicism. See also the **Mesa Public Library** a quarter-mile west at 2400 Central Avenue. Designed by Antoine Predock, New Mexico's most prominent architect, it ignited a storm of controversy when it was finished in 1994. Said one county council member, "When you build sculpture like this, it is hard to know if you have something that is going to bite you in the rear end." Like all of Predock's buildings, this library is intellectually challenging, laden with symbolism—such as a circular "kiva" that serves as a children's reading room and gathering place—but ultimately beautiful. The library's western wall features a curving window with stunning views of the Jémez Mountains.

Another Los Alamos attraction is the **Larry R. Walkup Aquatic Center** at 2760 Canyon Road, an Olympic-size indoor swimming pool. The Italian, Canadian, and Australian swim teams have trained here, appreciating the 7,410-foot elevation for its contribution to lung endurance. Amateur swimmers are welcome every day; there is a small admission fee.

❖

A quick detour to the north will take you to the ancient **Puye Cliff Dwellings**. These ruins, situated atop and in a 200-foot cliff of volcanic tuff, are on the Santa Clara Indian Reservation about 10 miles west of Santa Clara Pueblo. The occupants are believed to have migrated north from the rather more scenic Pajarito Plateau around A.D. 1250, then abandoned the Puye site in the mid-1500s. The Santa Clarans consider the people of Puye to be their direct ancestors. This isn't one of the more spectacular prehistoric pueblos in New Mexico, but it's well worth a visit for ruins enthusiasts. To reach the ruins drive north on NM 30. At the sign for Santa Clara Pueblo, follow the road about six miles. The entrance to the Puye Cliff Dwellings is on the right; call (505) 753-7326.

Puye Cliff Dwellings.

❖

Your next stop should be **Bandelier National Monument,** 11 miles south of Los Alamos. Extraordinary pueblo ruins are accessible here, although much of the 75-mile system of hiking trails has been closed since the forest fire of April 1996.

The ruins were discovered one October day in 1880, when a Swiss-born geologist named Adolph Bandelier peered over the rim of Frijoles Canyon 20 miles northwest of Santa Fe and saw something that would change the course of his life: the ruins of stone houses at least half a millennium old. Southwestern archaeology did not then exist, but over the next two decades Bandelier, along with a Swedish naturalist named Gustaf Nordenskiold and a Colorado cowboy named Richard Wetherill, would invent it. Thirty-six years later the forested Pajarito Plateau and the dramatic canyon that so captivated Bandelier would become a national monument, named in his honor.

This was evidently a good place to live in prehistoric times; there is evidence of human presence on the plateau and in the canyon since 9500 B.C. The canyon's year-round creek was obviously its key attraction throughout the millennia. The pueblo ruins of Frijoles Canyon, however, date from about A.D. 1175 to 1500.

There is no way to guess whether the ancient Anasazi who lived here were also enchanted by the canyon's stunning natural beauty, but modern visitors certainly are. In fall the box elder and narrow-leaf cottonwood trees flanking the stream explode with color. In summer the canyon is a moist, green, cool oasis. In winter—well, at an elevation of 6,066 feet the shivering residents of Frijoles Canyon would have anxiously awaited the first signs of spring.

The canyon's largest ruin is Tyuonyi, an oval-shaped pueblo built of roughly shaped volcanic tuff stones. Its construction took about a century, beginning around 1350. At its peak it had 400 rooms on several levels. And it would have had a defensive, forbidding attitude: the rooms completely encircle the large central plaza, and there was only one ground-floor entrance—which had large poles installed in it in a zigzag pattern, suggesting a maze. Today, however, the ruin is oddly beautiful, hugging the earth, its remaining walls a muted rainbow of salmon, auburn, gray, and black stones.

Several cliff dwellings hug the south-facing canyon wall along a 1.5-mile self-guided trail. Visitors in good physical condition also should climb the ladders 140 feet up to Ceremonial Cave, a reconstructed *kiva* in a large natural alcove in the canyon wall.

From Los Alamos take NM 501 west. At the junction with NM 4 turn left and continue 6 miles to Bandelier's entrance; (505) 672-3861. Call first as Bandelier may ban auto travel into the canyon.

❖

From Bandelier, continue west on NM 4 into the Jémez (pronounced HAY-mes) Mountains. On the right, about ten miles from Bandelier, notice **Valle Grande** ("Big Valley"), one of the largest calderas—a crater formed by a volcano's collapse—in the world. Fourteen miles across, it looks like an immense meadow in the shape of a saucer. Stop at **Jémez Falls**, where the Jémez River squeezes through a rocky chute and tumbles about 30 feet into a miniature canyon, widening into a wonderful bridal-veil spray as it falls.

Bares in the woods: the Forest Service is squeamish about publicizing this, but there are half a dozen hot springs in the Jémez Mountains that are popular with bathers—who customarily are nude. The most popular is **Spence Hot Springs,** 6.5 miles north of the Jémez Springs ranger station. There is no sign. If you're driving from Bandelier, watch for the Dark Canyon sign, then continue a quarter mile and look for a large dirt parking area on the left. The trail descends about 150 feet to the Jémez River, then up about 100 feet to a cauldron of natural hot water elegantly embraced by boulders. Most bathe in the buff, but more modest people can simply strip off their shoes and relax their feet in the hot water—nobody seems to care. In response to recent reports of a rare "brain-eating" amoeba in the hot springs, signs now warn bathers to avoid immersing their heads in the water. This guidebook, therefore, recommends caution as well, although rangers at the nearby ranger station told us that brain-eating amoeba can be in any hot springs, and that while 120 cases have been reported worldwide and 34 in the United States, none, *so far,* have been reported here.

Thirty miles west of Los Alamos are **Jémez Springs** and **Jémez State Monument,** a ruined pueblo and mission church. Jémez Springs, the town, has a health spa that mixes massage therapy and long baths in the hot mineral waters of the springs. There are private and group tubs, and the water includes natural traces of acid carbonate, calcium, potassium, and several other minerals said to contribute to a bather's well-being. The monument is not terrifically compelling. All that's left of the fourteenth-century pueblo of Giusewa is earthen mounds and a *kiva.* Walls of the 1621 church of San José de los Jémez remain. One fascinating observation is that the stone masonry of the Indian *kiva* and the Catholic church are almost identical. A Jémez Pueblo Indian working at the monument told me that the same people—the women and children of the pueblo—constructed both. "We used to have a sign that said that," he said, "but some women objected and we took it down."

To complete this round trip, continue south on NM 4. At San Ysidro follow NM 44 south and east, then turn north on Interstate 25 and return to Santa Fe.

■ TENT ROCKS, OLD TOWN ALBUQUERQUE, AND ÁCOMA PUEBLO

This excursion conveniently combines an easy hike in an unusual canyon, a visit to petroglyphs, a spin through an old historic town, and a tour of one of the Southwest's most remarkable historic pueblos. It's a fairly long drive, about 280 miles, so you might consider an overnight stay in Albuquerque.

❖

Tent Rocks (located southwest of Santa Fe off NM 22) describes itself. A million years ago, give or take a few, a volcanic eruption created a formation of soft

Tent Rocks in the Jémez Mountains (above) provide one of the most spectacular environments for hiking in the region. Less known, but even more unusual, is the Bisti Badlands (opposite), south of Farmington, where giant mushroom-shaped spires are set in the eerie desolation of a wild moonscape. Once a shallow sea, the area is rich in fossils.

pumice and tuff. Some of the rock eroded into conical tent-like formations that now poke into the sky, forming the walls of an intimate canyon. Some of the formations are almost comical: where caprock remains atop the softer cones, the effect is like a giant mushroom skewered by a teepee.

The hike is most spectacular, however, where the canyon narrows into a virtual slot as little as three feet wide and 100 feet deep. The trail hugs the canyon floor, and on a windless day the stillness inside the canyon is breathtaking. The one sound you may periodically hear is the tuff and pumice eroding, a pebble or two at a time. Watch for snakes and stay out of the canyon if a thunderstorm threatens. This is a bad place to be in a flash flood.

The trail demands no climbing, and it's only a three-mile round trip—an ideal introduction to hiking in New Mexico.

❖

Petroglyph National Monument, just off Interstate 25 heading south to Albuquerque, preserves some 15,000 images pecked into a lava escarpment by early Indian cultures. Some of the petroglyphs are suspected to be Archaic, as old as 2,000 to 3,000 years. But the most vivid ones are startlingly clear and refined images of birds, other animals, humans, and abstractions left by late-arriving Puebloans after A.D. 1300. Three easy, self-guided trails visit the best rock art in the monument.

Interpreting prehistoric art is a risky enterprise. Theories abound, and even modern Pueblo Indians who "read" their ancestors' rock art differ in their interpretations. Some signs almost surely track clan migrations, some might have been engraved prayers or curses, some may have served as solar calendars, some could be abstract art or casual graffiti. A visit here resolves no mysteries, but it is like touring a prehistoric art museum.

From Santa Fe take Interstate 25 south about 56 miles, then take Interstate 40 west to Coors Road exit north. Turn left on Atrisco Drive, which becomes Unser Boulevard. The monument is at 6900 Unser Boulevard; (505) 839-4429.

❖

Albuquerque's Old Town is a terrific arts shopping center and a mecca for sharp-eyed architecture buffs. Most of the buildings date from the nineteenth century, and several of them tell the story of Anglo pioneers struggling to reconcile their Greco-Roman architectural heritage with the adobe building blocks of Hispanic New Mexico.

Old Town is easy to find. Exit I-40 at Rio Grande Avenue and drive about half a mile south. Street parking is available in Old Town, and there are also municipal lots to the north and east.

La Villa de San Francisco de Alburquerque was founded in 1706. Christened after a Spanish viceroy, the Duke of Alburquerque, the city's name has been misspelled for at least a hundred years. Although movements are afoot to rectify the situation, undertaking to spell the duke's name properly on maps, official documents, and public buildings would be a formidable task.

Through most of the eighteenth century Albuquerque was just a loose string of farms and ranches flanking the Rio Grande, but in 1779 Santa Fe ordered the residents to begin forming a compact community, defensible against Apache attacks, around the church of San Felipe de Neri. This was the genesis of Old Town.

Old Town failed to become downtown Albuquerque because in 1880 the railroad passed a mile and a half to the east to avoid the nuisance of curving the track. Downtown blossomed around the railroad. Old Town briefly became a saloon and red-light district, but in the 1930s came a renaissance. Today it is delightful, if not thoroughly authentic.

Not authentic? Well, a few buildings have suffered "Puebloization" for the sake of touristization. Check the 1879 **Antonio Vigil House** at 413 Romero Street. Notice the *vigas*—ceiling beams protruding from intersecting walls—that would, if real, collide at right angles inside the house. They're fake. Real *vigas* jut north and south, or east and west, but never intersect.

Some other buildings poignantly illustrate the Anglo pioneers' yearning to make New Mexico look like home. **Our Lady of the Angels School,** built in 1877 as Albuquerque's first public school, mates Greek Revival to adobe vernacular. Several other buildings express little classical details, like modest carpenter's pediments over the windows. Spotting these architectural oddments in Old Town is a fascinating game.

Facing the plaza is Old Town's centerpiece, the 1793 church of **San Felipe de Neri** (which replaced an earlier structure). Its style is best described as French Carpenter Gothic executed, amazingly, in adobe. It claims to be the third oldest church in the United States that has had continuous services since its founding. (There are 800 families in the parish today.) The adjacent plaza, refreshingly, still serves its ancient civic function. Neighborhood residents relax on the benches, read newspapers, and feed pigeons, ignoring the tourist traffic. This feels like the spiritual center of Albuquerque, much more than its anonymous downtown.

There are about two dozen galleries in Old Town, along with many more boutiques, jewelry stores, and restaurants. Recommendation: **Agape Southwest Pueblo Pottery**, 414 Romero Street, one of the most comprehensive Indian pottery galleries in the Southwest.

The **Albuquerque Museum**, 2000 Mountain Road NW, is adjacent to Old Town and is decidedly worth a visit. It focuses mainly on New Mexico art, culture, and history. Guided walking tours of Old Town start from the Museum Tuesdays through Sundays from mid-April through October.

A hand-tinted photograph of Ácoma Pueblo produced around 1900 by the Detroit Photographic Company. (Underwood Archives, San Francisco)

Ácoma Pueblo (west of Albuquerque on Interstate 40) is romantically but not inaccurately termed the "Sky City" for its dramatic pose atop a 367-foot-high mesa. It also is sometimes called the oldest continuously occupied settlement in America, a distinction challenged by the Hopi village of Old Oraibi in Arizona. Actually, neither village can be dated to the precise year of its founding; published dates for Ácoma range from A.D. 1150 to the late 1200s. Venerable enough, at any rate.

The site evidently was chosen for defense. In 1541, one of Coronado's parties came across it and reported that "The natives . . . came down to meet us peacefully,

Ácoma Pueblo, sometimes called the "Sky City," rests atop a 367-foot-high mesa, as this aerial taken in the 1930s shows. (Underwood Archives, San Francisco)

although they might have spared themselves the trouble and remained on their rock, for we would not have been able to disturb them in the least." Ironic words, because half a century later the Spaniards were to disturb these Pueblo people in a shockingly cruel fashion.

Juan de Oñate's party marched up the mesa in 1598 and extracted the usual pledge of allegiance from the residents to the king. Later that year, as another Spanish party camped below the Sky City, a battle ensued and the Ácomas prevailed. A furious Oñate dispatched a larger force to teach the Indians a lesson. That they did. Hundreds of Indians were killed and hundreds more were taken prisoners. The Spaniards then cut off one foot of each captive man to serve as a "deterrent" to any future rebelliousness, and sentenced all the prisoners, male and female, to 20 years as slaves to Oñate's soldiers.

A little surprisingly, the pueblo in modern times welcomes visitors, although they must be escorted by an Ácoma guide. There are 465 houses atop the mesa, but only 13 families still live there—most Ácomas occupy more convenient houses scattered across the valley floor.

The architectural centerpiece of the town is the mission church of **San Esteban del Rey,** completed in 1640. It's another of those wonderful New Mexican missions that is almost more sculpture than architecture: pure, bold, unadorned form. It is the adobe Parthenon of this desert acropolis. Inside, the church walls feature not only the traditional Stations of the Cross, but also symbolic native art, such as an ear of corn growing under a benevolent rainbow.

The Sky City's houses may not delight historic-preservation purists. Although they still lack twentieth-century amenities such as electricity, plumbing, and phones, they have been adapted to some modern needs with screen doors and milled casement windows. A few, incongruously, have second stories of concrete block set over adobe first stories. There are seven square *kivas,* all built above ground—that, our guide said, was a ruse to fool the Spaniards into thinking they were mere houses so the Ácomas could carry on their religion in secret.

There is a charge for the guided tour, and an additional charge for taking still pictures. No video cameras are allowed. Before visiting call the Ácoma Tourist Visitor Center: (505) 470-4967 or (800) 747-0181.

Ácoma is known for its feast day rooster pull which involves Ácoma horsemen galloping past roosters buried in sand up to their necks and reaching down to pull them up by the head. Protests by animal rights activists may cause the Ácoma to close the feast day to outsiders.

■ WEST TO CHACO CANYON

Chaco Culture National Historical Park is a long drive from Santa Fe. As the crow flies—more about crows later—this incredible collection of ruins is 112 miles to the west. Unfortunately, all the road routes snake roundabout, none less than 180 miles, and over 20 miles of this is unpaved. Leave Santa Fe before dawn, arrive early at Chaco, and plan to spend all day, but preferably not overnight. Pack lunch and plenty of water; there are no concessions.

The prehistoric ruins of Chaco Canyon are the most monumental, perplexing, and controversial anywhere in what we now call the United States. At least a dozen books have been written about them, each proposing different answers to the question that keeps Anasazi archaeology swirling in turmoil: What *was* Chaco?

We know this much: it was a terrifically inhospitable place for a prehistoric metropolis. In modern times the U.S. Park Service has recorded a high of 106° F, a low of -38° F, and an average of 8.7 sparse inches of rain a year. Yet between A.D. 900 and 1130, a march of monumental buildings—the largest, Pueblo Bonito, had between 600 and 800 rooms and 40 kivas—rose from the canyon floor. Archaeologists figure they could have housed up to 5,000 people, but the meager natural resources available near the desert canyon could not have supported more than a thousand. Moreover, these "great houses" were architect-designed in precise geometric forms (Pueblo Bonito is an immense "D" 500 feet long) and built with sandstone shaved into remarkably precise bricks. Nothing like this had appeared anywhere in the American Southwest before. Who or what inspired it? Still more: Absolutely straight dirt "roads," most a uniform 30 feet wide and visible today from the air when the sun is low in the sky, radiated from Chaco to outlying communities up to 42 miles distant. Why would people who had no draft animals or wheeled vehicles need freeways?

An eight-mile loop road visits seven of the 11 great houses in the canyon, including Pueblo Bonito, the most spectacular. I strongly recommend the trail ascending to the canyon rim behind the ruin of Kin Kletso, which provides crow's-eye floor-plan views of three of the great ruins. The trail is only mildly strenuous, but carry water and watch out for rattlesnakes.

And crows. Very strange things happen here, as park rangers will confirm. An acquaintance of mine, hiking in Chaco Canyon, once followed a crow. The bird fluttered down onto a prehistoric stone axe. "It was like it was meant for me," the hiker said. He took it home as a souvenir (illegal as well as unwise). Within the next six months his restaurant business began to collapse, and he developed skin rashes that couldn't be diagnosed. Then one day he rolled out of bed to answer the phone and the stone severed his achilles tendon. "There was a *lot* of blood," he said.

The next week he drove 500 miles to Chaco to return the stone. He then told me about a conversation he'd had with a Chaco park ranger: "He was a very rational guy, but when I told him about the crow he turned sheet-white. He said, 'You didn't follow it, did you? You just don't follow crows. Crows are messengers from another world.'"

From Santa Fe take Interstate 25 south 41 miles to NM 44. Follow NM 44 north about 120 miles to County Road 7900 (3 miles east of Nageezi), then head south along NM 57. Well-marked signs point the way to Chaco Canyon; (505) 786-7014.

(opposite) Pueblo Bonito of Chaco Canyon. (following pages) A kiva at Pecos National Historical Park.

CUISINE ❖ RESTAURANTS

> MONROE'S NEW MEXICAN FOOD
> GRILLED SALMON TONIGHT
>
> —*Restaurant sign, Santa Fe's Cerrillos Road*

WHAT, NEW MEXICAN SALMON? Lost, somehow, 1,200 miles upstream in the Rio Grande? No, what's lost here is New Mexican food, now spawning offshoots as exotic as buffalo sausage and blue crab, bathed in sauces incorporating everything from papaya juice to puréed *piñon* nuts and served with polenta or *risotto* and accompanied by chile-spiked beer or margaritas made with tequila and Grand Marnier. Don't believe it? Here's a sampler from contemporary Santa Fe menus:

> *Rabbit confit enchilada with molé poblano sauce and orange-jicama salsa (Coyote Cafe)*
> *Green chile brioche French toast with sautéed spiced pears and persimmon compote with wild boar bacon (SantaCafe)*
> *Sassafras wood-smoked quails with jicama, grilled red-banana papaya-lime salsa, and achiote cream (Corn Dance Cafe)*
> *Grilled salmon burrito with goat cheese and cucumber salsa (Cafe Pasqual's)*
> *Grilled tofu and vegetable fajitas (Old Mexico Grill)*

Tofu *fajitas!* Nowhere but Santa Fe will the diner encounter such wild and crazy permutations—many will say perversions—of traditional New Mexican food. At the same time, nowhere else is the nova of New Southwestern cuisine flaming so brightly. Culinary experimentation is at epidemic levels. Not all of it is successful, but one thing every foodie can agree on: Santa Fe is an outrageously interesting place to eat.

Somewhere close to 175 restaurants are listed in the Santa Fe phone directory, not counting chain eateries. Choices are as varied as any big city, including Spanish tapas, Chinese dim sum, Pacific Rim fusion, French, Italian, Thai, American Indian, Asian Indian—and even New Mexican.

"The tradition is still here," says Katherine Kagel, owner of the very popular Cafe Pasqual's, "but it's being lost. There's a whole group of cooks in town who won't let a chile walk through the door."

She seems overly pessimistic; there are still dozens of traditional New Mexican restaurants in town—restaurants that won't let a salmon walk through the door—and there are still some moms who patiently pat out damp corn *masa* into thin discs and make their own tortillas before every meal. Santa Fe's supermarkets routinely carry ingredients that are almost impossible to find even in other Southwestern cities with large Hispanic populations. The local Albertson's carries canned menudo (tripe soup), camarón (dried and shredded shrimp), and, of course, powdered Chimayó chile. Chile is not just an ingredient here, but a passion, and Santa Feans eat it *hot*. Incidentally, nothing will draw more derision around Santa Fe than to spell it or pronounce it *chili*, as in Texas. *Nuevo Mexicanos* use the correct Spanish spelling; it is a signature of the state.

It is also declassé to refer to the traditional dishes of Santa Fe such as *picadillo* and *carne adovada* as "Mexican food." The preferred term is New Mexican food. Santa Fe isn't just being snooty. There are real differences between the traditional Hispanic cooking of northern New Mexico and that elsewhere in the Southwest.

HARD WORK ON THE HACIENDA

Behind the style of the big river households there was much work, for the men out of doors, for the women within. . . . Food and drink took much work to produce. The women made spiced wine, simmered in an earthen pot for a day with spices and sugar, sealed with a ring of fresh dough. Sweet cookies were made with twenty-four egg yolks. On a heated metate stone, dense chocolate was made by grinding cocoa beans, stick cinnamon, pecans and maple sugar—all imported—into a paste which was dried and cut into cakes. Cooked with thick whole milk, these made the black chocolate drink which was served at breakfast, and at four in the afternoon with cookies. The finest tortillas—large, thin, round corncakes—were made from blue corn meal. Three of these, layered with slices of pink onion and curls of yellow cheese and sprinkled with green lettuce and swimming in cooked red chili pepper sauce, made a favorite dish. . . . Pork fat was diced and fried in deep fat to make cracklings which were used in place of bacon. A soupbone was used not once but many times, and was even passed from one poor family to another to boil with beans. In the fall . . . the hacienda women cut up sweet pumpkins and melons, setting the pieces out on stakes to dry.

—Paul Horgan, *Great River: The Rio Grande*, 1954

The reason is that until recently, Santa Fe and its environs remained relatively iso-lated and culturally unique, so its cuisine developed unique characteristics. Even as Anglos began streaming into the region in large numbers in the mid-twentieth cen-tury, the American "melting pot" didn't find its way to the stove here. "Simply put, the New Mexicans refused to melt," writes New Mexico historian Marc Simmons.

The Spaniards of the *Entrada* encountered a semi-arid land that yielded pre-cious little natural bounty when compared to southern Mexico or southern Eu-rope. Sixteenth-century Puebloans subsisted on a diet of cultivated corn, beans, and squash, supplemented with occasional wild game—much the same as their Anasazi and Mogollon forebears had done for a millennium. The Hispanic settlers introduced two important improvements: ranching, to provide a reliable source of meat; and chile, to flavor it. Still, until Mexican independence opened New Mexi-co to Yankee trade in 1821, Santa Fe cooking would have been fairly spare and primitive.

■ SANBUSCO MARKET

To get an insight into the farming traditions of the Rio Grande Valley, visit the Santa Fe Farmers' Market (Sanbusco Market Center, Tuesday and Saturday mornings,

Produce from Sanbusco Market includes squash (above) and freshly baked bread (opposite).

June through October). It's as much cultural reservoir as food market; some of the families selling produce out of pickups and campers have been working the same New Mexico land for six or seven generations. In one stall, a man roasts hundreds of green chiles in a rotating steel mesh drum heated by roaring propane jets made from recycled tin cans. (The aroma is delectable.) Another is selling miniature decorative corn in a mosaic of white, yellow, cherry, and purple kernels. There is apple cider (100% organic, made last night), homemade salsas and chutneys, apples, squashes, tomatoes, lettuce, onions, and herbs. Free samples abound, and they definitely generate sales. This *is* a tradition in jeopardy: all across northern New Mexico, old family farms are under pressure from higher taxes, developers, and a new generation that's uninterested in farming.

■ NEW TRENDS IN NEW MEXICAN CUISINE

Through the first three-quarters of this century, the glory of Santa Fe food was basic but delicious traditional New Mexican dishes: enchiladas, chiles rellenos, tamales, carne asada, carne adovada, simmered beans, posole. Nobody fretted about cholesterol, nor about which chile might best flavor a papaya-tangerine sauce for pheasant breast. Local sources dispute exactly when and how the nuevo New Mexican (or nouvelle Numex) era began, but Mark Miller's famous Coyote Cafe, born in 1987, certainly had something to do with it. Miller conjoined ingredients and techniques from Mexico, New Mexico, France, and Berkeley, drew a gush of national publicity and the suspicion of local traditionalists, and inspired a rash of innovation.

Too much, possibly? "I don't think Santa Fe cuisine has a direction now," said Cafe Pasqual's Kagel. "Restaurateurs are very independent. This is the kind of place now that's going to continue to attract chefs from other parts of the world, and they're going to bring what they do to Santa Fe." Added John O'Brien, owner of Atalaya Restaurant & Bakery, "I don't know what more anyone could do with Santa Fe food now. People in the business wonder if the whole Southwestern craze is about to play itself out."

Answer: probably. Today's culinary trends rarely last a generation. It's a safe wager, however, that whatever happens in Santa Fe kitchens, chile will be the cornerstone of it.

SANTA FE SCHOOL OF COOKING

Janet Mitchell is plopping red chiles into her *carne adovada* sauce, tuning the ensemble like a composer choosing among saxes, bassoons, and trombones, looking for the exact mixture of finesse and snarl the music needs. Her basic instrument is Chimayó chile, grown around the town of the same name 40 miles north of Santa Fe. "You can use more Chimayó for more flavor without increasing the heat," she says. "*Caribe* chiles turn up the heat. *Anchos* add richness and smokiness."

"It's like wine," she adds, as the aroma from the open saucepan storms the room. "You can talk about chiles in terms of smoke, or licorice, or plum. I think there are about 300 adjectives to describe the flavors of chiles."

This is a weekday morning class at the Santa Fe School of Cooking, and 17 of us from assorted parts of the country have assembled to learn some of northern New Mexico's traditional culinary secrets. It operates in a sunny second-story room in a retail marketplace a block from Santa Fe's 385-year-old plaza. Owner Susan Curtis started it in 1989, reasoning that a lot of people come to Santa Fe mainly to eat, and a school would give visitors a way to take the city's flavors home.

It began with one instructor and one class, and it's now six instructors and a dozen classes. There are three in traditional northern New Mexican cuisine, and others in Spanish *tapas*, low-fat Mexican cooking, and contemporary Southwestern. In summer, the high season, 100 to 120 people take the classes every week.

It's also a retail store, which manager Nicole Curtis, Susan's daughter, says is a perfect complement to the classes. Participants typically leave the store with armloads of spices and herbs like *epazote* (which cuts the antisocial after-effects of pinto beans) as well as chile varieties such as *guajillo, chipotle, moritas,* and *cascabeles,* all as easily available as moon rocks in most of the country. There's mail order to supply New Mexican food fanatics stranded in, say . . . New Hampshire.

Our class menu today covers a lot of culinary ground: *carne adovada, calabacitas* (corn and squash), *chiles rellenos,* homemade tortillas, refried beans, and *sopaipillas.* This is definitely not an American Heart Association-approved feast, but Mitchell does compromise by subbing vegetable oil for lard—which in *adovada,* with its pervasive red chile sauce, will make no difference in flavor.

Carne adovada translates best as "cured meat," and it dates from New Mexico's pre-fridge days. Strips of pork are marinated in the chile sauce for 24 hours, then stewed in the same sauce. The marinating not only flavors the meat, but keeps bacteria at bay. Not every organism loves chile.

(continues)

As she cooks, Mitchell tosses out a wealth of helpful hints and chile lore. "Hispanic cooks believe that if you cut the meat with the grain it will absorb more of the sauce, which will tenderize it." On *chiles rellenos*: "The Anaheim you get everywhere else is the same variety as the New Mexico Hatch, but California's mild climate doesn't develop the intense flavor in the chile." On making tortillas: "They don't have to be perfectly round. They should look like they were made by the human hand." That's reassurance for her assistant, Matt Gomez, who is new to the tortilla craft, and some of his are coming out shaped like Nevada. "Just don't overcook them, or they'll taste like Frisbees. Basically, you only want to dry them out."

The whole demonstration takes two hours—much of the instructors' prep work is done in advance—and then we all prepare to eat it. The aromas alone could arouse de Anza from his grave; even the humid scent of freshly griddled tortillas evokes warmly satisfying images of mom, hearth, home. Factory-prepared Mexican foods don't even come close. These dishes are a bunch of trouble to cook, but the results are worth it.

And when we eat, we are warmed (in more ways than one) and gratified. It isn't just the lingering tang of the chile concerto on our tongues. It's also the echo of history, the notion that we visitors are learning traditions perpetuated by people whose roots in New Mexico stretch back to the sixteenth century.

"The traditional New Mexican cuisine has been here forever," declares Susan Curtis. "It will never die."

Santa Fe School of Cooking, 116 W. San Francisco Street, Santa Fe 87501; (505) 983-4511. Classes offered year-round. Reservations are advisable.

Janet Mitchell of the Santa Fe School of Cooking.

Ristras *decorate adobe wall at Rancho de las Golondrinas.*

■ CHILES

There are more than 300 varieties of chiles and a universe of things one can do with them. They can be used fresh, pickled, dried, smoked, crushed, or powdered. A whole pod or several can be simmered all day in a stew to impart a distinctive flavor—and different varieties do have different flavors. A *chipotle,* which is a smoked jalapeño, will invest the pot with both smoke and fire, while an *ancho* has a plum-like flavor. Even greater differences exist in the fire quotient, which comes from an alkaloid chemical called capsaicin that develops naturally in the chile. This is measured scientifically in Scoville Units, a scale developed by a Parke-Davis chemist in 1912. The drug company was marketing a chile-based ointment for arthritis sufferers, and while some were enjoying relief, others were getting blisters, so a test was needed to quantify the relative power of different chiles.

An everyday bell pepper will rate close to zero Scoville Units, a jalapeño typically will score about 5,000, and an *habanero* up to *300,000!* Eating an *habanero,* a brilliant orange chile about the size of a stubby thumb, is like grabbing a mouthful of live killer bees. Carelessly rub your eye after fingering one, and it will put an end to productive work for the rest of the day.

New Mexicans, unlike the Texans they love to hate, seldom eat their chiles straight. Instead, they're commonly incorporated into *salsas,* or sauces.

The first thing an outlander needs to know is the meaning of the question "Red or green?" which usually follows any order of a traditional New Mexican plate. It means red or green sauce, which is slathered over burritos, chiles rellenos, enchiladas, omelets—practically everything but salmon. Red is made with dried chiles, green with fresh. Before freezers and trucks from California, green was the summer sauce, and red warmed New Mexico's palates through the winter. Both now are made year-round. Green tends to be hotter. It is made mostly or entirely with Hatch chiles, grown in southwestern New Mexico. Hatches are the same species as the familiar Anaheims from southern California, but New Mexico's cool summer nights urge the chile to develop more capsaicin.

In New Mexico, chiles find their way into some strange places. The microbrewery at Embudo Station 40 miles north of Santa Fe offers a green chile ale that intriguingly mingles the sensations of good, cold brew with the fires of hell as it trickles through the throat. Brewmaster Brandon Santos explains that he simply dumps roasted green chiles into the fermentation vats with pale ale for three days, then filters out the vegetable matter.

Chiles find their way onto New Mexican breakfast plates, which isn't strange at all. New Mexican breakfasts are infinitely better than the bowls of steaming limp gray stuff that greets too many American palates in the morning. *Huevos rancheros* is one popular staple: eggs poached in a red chile sauce, served over corn tortillas and dripping with melted cheese. Breakfast burros (burritos) are unpredictable but delicious. At El Taoseño in Taos, they can be a bacon-and-egg scramble swaddled in a flour tortilla; at Tia Sophia in Santa Fe, expect shredded potatoes and bacon wrapped in a flour tortilla and drenched in an eye-opening green chile sauce.

■ TORTILLAS

Visitors also need a reverent appreciation of the tortilla, the staff of life from northern New Mexico all the way to Central America. Indians made tortillas long before the arrival of Columbus and Coronado, grinding dried corn with a *mano* and *metate* (essentially a stone mortar and pestle), mixing in a little water and heating it. Tortillas made from wheat flour are a relatively modern invention, probably issuing from northern Mexico in the nineteenth century. Blue corn tortillas may or may not have been made in prehistoric times, but they have become a virtual symbol of trendy Santa Fe cuisine in the last decade. And now come *flavored* tortillas, invention of Leona Tiede, who runs a little burrito stand next to the Santuario de Chimayó. "One of the B&Bs wanted something besides toast and croissants to serve for breakfast," she said, "so I tried making cinnamon tortillas and it kind of went crazy from there." Crazy? Try 22 flavors.

The tortilla's uses are even more varied than leavened bread's. They can be eaten plain with butter or salsa, filled with cheese and heated (a *quesadilla*), rolled around a filling of meat or beans (a burrito), fried and wrapped around a filling (a taco), or cut into triangles and fried as chips to dip in *salsa*. They take the place of pasta in Mexican chicken soup. When they're served at plateside in a covered basket, you should tear them into smaller pieces, dump a lump of stew or beans inside, and use the tortilla to ferry food to mouth. As with leavened bread, freshness is everything. A tortilla that's been snoring in the refrigerator for three days might as well be a compact disk. If you stumble across a restaurant that's making its own tortillas in the kitchen several times a day, forget the New Mexican scallops in ancho-garlic-cilantro butter over at La Maison del Rio Grande, and savor the former. It's for real.

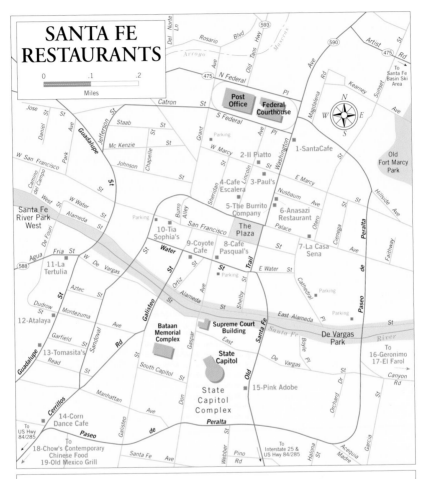

SANTA FE RESTAURANTS

0   .1   .2
Miles

Anasazi Restaurant 6

Atalaya 12

Burrito Company 5

Cafe Escalera 4

Cafe Pasqual's 8

Chow's Contemporary Chinese Food 18

Corn Dance Cafe 14

Coyote Cafe 9

El Farol 17

Geronimo 16

Il Piatto 2

La Casa Sena 7

La Tertulia 11

Old Mexico Grill 19

Paul's 3

Pink Adobe 15

SantaCafe 1

Tia Sophia's 10

Tomasita's 13

■ SANTA FE AREA RESTAURANTS

> *P*rices per person, excluding tax, tip, and drinks
> $=under $10 per person; $$=$10–$20; $$$= over $20

☆ Recommended by author

SANTA FE

☆ **Anasazi Restaurant.** 113 Washington Ave.; (505) 988-3236. $$$
Both decor and cuisine would make a prehistoric Anasazi think he'd gone to another world. Modern foodies may think they've gone to heaven. Complicated, innovative, and beautifully prepared New Southwestern dishes may mingle, for example, venison, dried cherries, and pumpkin. Elegant, but nobody demands you dress up. Santa Fe's best restaurant.

✗ **Atalaya Restaurant & Bakery.** 320 S. Guadalupe St.; (505) 982-2709. $–$$
A thoroughly charming cafe with a cozy brick interior and a lovely outdoor patio. The innovative menu features the season's freshest offerings along with delicious homemade pastries and bread. Prices are refreshingly reasonable.

☆ **The Burrito Company.** 111 Washington Ave.; (505) 982-4453. $
Authentic New Mexican food on a budget actually exists downtown, served sans fanfare

Coyote Cafe is perhaps Santa Fe's most famous restaurant.

on paper plates. Atmosphere comes with the sidewalk tables, set out for a view of the Palace of the Governors. Ample and fiery plates of red chile burritos or enchiladas and *posole* are a bargain.

✗ **Cafe Escalera.** 130 Lincoln Ave.; (505) 989-8188. $$$

Manhattan-meets-Santa Fe. The decor here is urban-minimalist with little to distract patrons from the savory, contemporary fare elegantly displayed on their plates. The menu changes constantly to spotlight seasonal specialties. Wine list nicely compliments the food.

✯ **Cafe Pasqual's.** 121 Don Gaspar Ave.; (505) 983-9340. $$

Fresh ingredients always, a sunny dining room with cheerful hand-painted tiles, and an outrageously eclectic menu draw-

Katherine Kagel, owner of Pasqual's.

ing inspiration from New Mexican, Chinese, Thai, and owner Katherine Kagel's Jewish grandmother's cooking make this one of Santa Fe's most inspired small restaurants. Smuggle all this home; buy her cookbook on your way out.

✯ **Chow's Contemporary Chinese Food.** 720 St. Michael's Dr.; (505) 471-7120. $$

"Contemporary" is the key word here, since most American Chinese food is anything but. With innovations such as scallops in jade sauce (made with ginger, green onion, cilantro, and spinach), Chow's wows. Cheerful service, unusually high-quality fortunes in the cookies.

✯ **Corn Dance Cafe.** 1501 Paseo de Peralta (inside the Hotel Santa Fe); (505) 982-1200. $$–$$$

Here's a fascinating concept: Traditional Native American cooking dressed up with fancy contemporary techniques. Emphasis is on wood-grilled seafood and meats and healthful eating—owner Loretta Barrett Oden, a member of the Potawatomi tribe, points out that buffalo, which appears in several guises on her menu, is even lower in cholesterol than chicken.

✯ **Coyote Cafe.** 132 E. Water St.; (505) 983-1615. $$$

Very popular. Very noisy. And very controversial. Some conservative Santa Feans resent the fame Mark Miller's restaurant has drawn, because it caused the eclipse of traditional New Mexican cuisine, at least in

Mark Miller, chef and owner of Coyote Cafe.

the national consciousness. Rabbit enchiladas with *molé poblano* and orange-jicama salsas? Radical indeed, but Coyote's food is superb. Expensive *prix fixe* except for weekend brunch.

✩ **El Farol.** 808 Canyon Rd.;
   (505) 983-9912. **$$**
What could be more appropriate than Spanish cuisine in the old Spanish capital? Specialty at El Farol ("The Lantern") are tapas—appetizer-sized plates of Spanish specialties such as shrimp sautéed with garlic, sherry, and lime juice. Good Spanish wine list, entertainment nightly.

✩ **Geronimo.** 724 Canyon Rd.;
   (505) 982-1500. **$$–$$$**
No connection to the famed Apache warrior here, but a man named Gerónimo Lopez did own this house for a time around the mid-18th century. There's nothing historic about the cuisine, however, which includes New Southwestern dishes such as blackened

red snapper tossed with pasta, smoked tomato and *chipotle* chile sauce.

✩ **Il Piatto.** 95 W. Marcy St.;
   (505) 984-1091. **$$**
The decor is a thousand kitchen implements hung on the walls, which correctly focuses diners' minds on what's important in this rightly celebrated new bistro: the food. *Esquire* rated this one of America's best new restaurants in 1996. Pasta, roast chicken, grilled seafood, liberal herbal seasoning.

La Casa Sena is actually two restaurants in one.

✩ **La Casa Sena.** 125 E. Palace Ave.;
   (505) 988-9232. **$$–$$$**
Two restaurants here: a stylish and expensive place serving northern New Mexican crossed with *nuevo,* and a crowded cantina with simpler and cheaper food and superb young musicians who sing Broadway show tunes and wait tables. Try an alfresco lunch in the plaza; the cantina for a fun evening.

Taco with rice and beans (top). Chiles rellenos *(above).*
Carne adovada *with* sopaipillas *(opposite).*

✰ **La Tertulia.** 416 Agua Fria; (505) 988-2769. $$

This pretty restaurant housed in a historic adobe Dominican convent offers traditional tamales and *adovada* and some more modern creations, but turns back before the "nuevo" border. Lace tablecloths under all these chile sauces are an impractical but graceful touch. Reservations requested.

✰ **Old Mexico Grill.** 2434 Cerrillos Rd.; (505) 473-0338. $$

As the name suggests, this restaurant serves Mexican, not New Mexican food—for example, a salad of shrimp on lettuce, jicama, and oranges, or roast chicken smothered in a sauce of *serrano* chile, peanuts, pumpkin, and sesame seeds. Serious Mexican cuisine, not common in the United States.

The chef at Old Mexico Grill.

✰ **Paul's.** 72 W. Marcy St.; (505) 982-8738. $$

Look around; you'll know you're in Santa Fe: wooden lizards and snakes roam the peach-painted walls, chickens painted like dalmatians perch in the windows. But the new American food is as serious as the decor is playful—like the salmon baked in a crust of crushed pecans and bathed in sorrel sauce. Good value.

✗ **Pink Adobe.** 406 Old Santa Fe Trail; (505) 983-7712. $$$

Housed in a 300-year-old building, former barracks for Spanish soldiers, "the Pink" is a landmark. Rosalea Murphey opened the doors 50 years ago, kicking off Santa Fe's outstanding culinary reputation. The menu offers standard fare: steaks, lamb, pork, and traditional New Mexican dishes.

✰ **SantaCafé.** 231 Washington Ave.; (505) 984-1788. $$$

This elegant restaurant has eclipsed the Coyote Cafe in national fame, offering a fusion-style cuisine of Asian, European, and New Mexican food. (Example: ginger-cured salmon on crispy won tons with tequila-citrus aioli.) Setting is the historic Padre Gallegos House, private (and palatial) residence of one of the priests defrocked by Bishop Lamy.

✰ **Tia Sophia's.** 210 W. San Francisco St.; (505) 983-9880. $

Best place to eat breakfast in Santa Fe. Arrive at 7, park without fear of a ticket, and order the breakfast burrito, *huevos rancheros,* or cheese enchiladas. Open for breakfast and lunch, not dinner.

✰ **Tomasita's.** 500 S. Guadalupe; (505) 983-5721. $

"Chile is a main ingredient of our dishes

and we serve it hot. If you are new to the taste please ask for a sample before ordering. . . ." So warns this traditional New Mexican restaurant's menu. Believe it: this may be the hottest New Mexican food in America. Tomasita's is hot commercially, too; it's Santa Fe's most popular restaurant. Huge crowds; go at some hour like 4:43 p.m. No reservations.

NEAR SANTA FE

☆ **Dim Sum—Then Some.**
Ten miles S. of Santa Fe on NM 14; (505) 474-4111. $–$$
Shanghai native Mimi Ho opened this restaurant way out in the country because, well, that happened to be where she lived. Stunning barbecued ribs, sesame noodles, shrimp-calamari minglings—not at all the usual parade of dumplings. Great value. Call first: usually open weekends only.

☆ **Embudo Station Restaurant and Brewery.**
Fifteen miles N. of Española on NM 68; (505) 852-4707. $–$$
A beautiful place nestled under ancient cottonwoods on the west bank, literally, of the Rio Grande. Succulent smoked meats and vividly flavored green chile beer from Embudo Station's own smokehouse and brewery. November through March Embudo Station is only open on the weekends.

✗ **Gabriel's.** 13 miles N. of Santa Fe off US 285; (505) 455-7000. $$
Expertly prepared Mexican and Southwest cuisine—the guacamole, made fresh at your table, is sheer genius. If you arrive

around sunset, try for a table on the outdoor patio, order a fabulous margarita, and take in the spectacular views of the Sangre de Cristo Mountains.

Serving up some of Gabriel's famous Mexican fare.

CHIMAYÓ
The town of Chimayó is located 25 miles north of Santa Fe on NM 520.

☆ **Rancho de Chimayó Restaurante.** NM 520 one mile S. of Chimayó; (505) 351-4444. $$
The Jaramillo family settled around present-day Chimayó in 1695; nine generations later their descendants run this prodigiously popular restaurant in a rambling nineteenth-century hacienda. How popular? Try 300,000 meals a year. Try also not to arrive at lunchtime in summer when tour buses are disgorging diners by the hundreds; strike at an odd hour. Excellent traditional New Mexican food.

TAOS

(For map of Taos restaurants see page 233)

✗ **AppleTree.** Taos Plaza; (505) 758-1900. $$$

A popular and pleasant restaurant with cozy fireside tables in the winter months and a breezy patio in the warmer seasons. The menu offers a range of dishes from curried chicken to shrimp quesadillas.

✗ **The Chow Cart.** 402 Paseo del Pueblo Sur; (505) 758-3632. $

Locals flock to this renovated '50s-style drive–thru for sensational *chiles rellenos* fried and wrapped in tortillas. Devour this brilliant creation in the privacy of your car or sit outside under the shady trees.

✿ **El Taoseño.** 819 Paseo del Pueblo Sur; (505) 758-4142. $

Tourists don't come here, but they should. The breakfast crowd arrives in pickups and cop cars and engorges big, cheap plates of *chorizo* and eggs, potatoes with green chile sauce, and *huevos rancheros*. There are "American" breakfasts here too, but Taoseños stare quizzically at people who order them.

✿ **Jacquelina's Southwestern Cuisine.** 1541 S. Paseo del Pueblo Sur; (505) 751-0399. $$

This is Taos's hottest feed bag at this writing, although the ambiance at one day's lunch was ruined for me by one diner who had the temerity to wear a coat and tie. Hey, guy, this is Taos! The menu weaves through traditional and *nuevo* New Mexican, both delectably executed.

✿ **Lambert's of Taos.** 309 Paseo del Pueblo Sur; (505) 758-1009. $$–$$$

This pretty, cottage-like restaurant serves new American cuisine such as grilled lamb chops with mushrooms, and slips in an occasional New Mexican accent with smoky *chipotle* sauces. Superb.

✿ **Marciano's Ristorante.** 112 Placita; (505) 751-0805. $$

This quiet, intimate, and unpretentious Italian cafe serves mostly pasta dishes, some spiked with chile. Emphasis is on organic vegetables and meats, homemade sauces, and a long wine and beer list. Very good; rather expensive for pasta.

✿ **Villa Fontana.** Five miles north of Taos on NM 522; (505) 758-5800. $$$

Owner-chef Carlo Gislimberti here serves up stunning northern Italian dishes such as piccata of venison with wild mushrooms bathed in vodka demi-glace. Service seems excessively formal for Taos, but diners in tattered jeans still are perfectly welcome.

Corn has been a staple of the Southwestern diet for centuries.

PRACTICAL INFORMATION

NOTE: Compass American Guides makes every effort to ensure the accuracy of its information; however, as conditions and prices change frequently, we recommend that readers also contact the local visitors bureaus for the most up-to-date information—see "Information Numbers" for more telephone numbers.

AREA CODE

All New Mexico answers to the (505) area code. Calls from Santa Fe to Tesuque, Los Alamos, and White Rock are local; everything else is long distance. Long distance calls made within New Mexico, as from outside, must include (505).

■ METRIC CONVERSIONS

1 foot = .305 meters
1 mile = 1.6 kilometers
Centigrade = Fahrenheit temp. minus 32, divided by 1.8

■ WHEN TO GO

No question about it: October is the best month to visit northern New Mexico. Summer's mad crowds have diminished—at least slightly—and the native cottonwoods, aspens, and alders are turning a brilliant gold. Brisk mornings and evenings call for sweaters, but winter's occasional blizzards are still well in the distance.

CLIMATE AVERAGES

| MONTH | FAHRENHEIT | | CENTIGRADE | | RAINFALL IN INCHES |
	High	Low	High	Low	(25 mm=1inch)
January	40°	19°	4°	-7°	.61"
February	44°	22°	7°	-6°	.79"
March	51°	28°	11°	-2°	.76"
April	60°	35°	16°	2°	.92"
May	69°	43°	21°	6°	1.18"
June	79°	52°	26°	11°	1.11"
July	82°	57°	28°	14°	2.41"
August	80°	56°	27°	13°	2.31"
September	74°	49°	23°	9°	1.65"
October	63°	38°	17°	3°	1.10"
November	50°	27°	10°	-2°	.72"
December	41°	20°	5°	-7°	.71"

Heavy winter snowfall is not uncommon. Here a foot of snow blankets the Santa Fe Plaza in 1912. (Museum of New Mexico)

If your aim is to enjoy Santa Fe with the smallest possible crowds, try November, the first three weeks of December, or January. Avoid times that coincide with the big annual events: Christmas, Spanish Market (July), Indian Market (August), and the opera season (July–August). Snow falls mainly December through March, which may make day trips into the Jémez or Sangre de Cristo mountains rather adventurous: you'll learn firsthand why so many Santa Feans have four-wheel drive.

Particularly in summer, apply a sunscreen if you're going to be spending time outdoors. It may not be hot, but ultraviolet radiation at these 7,000-foot elevations is very hazardous to the skin.

■ GETTING THERE

By Air. Most visitors coming to Santa Fe from substantial distances fly into Albuquerque, which has commercial airline service with a number of major carriers, then rent a car and drive the 60 freeway miles to Santa Fe. Santa Fe's small airport has commuter service (i.e., planes with propellers) with just one carrier, United Express, offering connections to Denver. Call (800) 241-6522 for reservations.

By Shuttle. A convenient way to make the Albuquerque–Santa Fe connection is to use **Shuttle Jack,** a bus service with eight to ten daily round trips between the Albuquerque airport and any Santa Fe motel or hotel (with advance reservations). Phone: (505) 243-3244 (in Albuquerque), or (505) 982-4311 (in Santa Fe). You can make phone reservations with a credit card.

By Train or Bus. Amtrak provides passenger train service to Albuquerque and Lamy, 15 miles southeast of Santa Fe, the latter with a bus shuttle into the city. Greyhound Bus Lines goes to Albuquerque, Santa Fe, and Taos.

■ GETTING AROUND

You need a detailed street map of Santa Fe. Absolutely. You have *nada* chance of negotiating Santa Fe's seventeenth-century tangle of asphalt linguine without one.

By Car. Do you need a car in Santa Fe? Admittedly, it can seem much more nuisance than convenience when trying to find a parking space. But unless you plan to confine your sightseeing to downtown and Canyon Road, it is hard to get by without personal wheels. One possibility: Take the Albuquerque–Santa Fe

(preceding pages) The sun sets over the rugged landscape of northwest New Mexico.

shuttle to your downtown hotel, spend the first couple of days on foot, and then rent a car for day-tripping. There are rental agencies downtown.

Bus service. Santa Fe does have a comprehensive city bus service, Santa Fe Trails, with six routes. Phone: (505) 820-6060 or (505) 984-6730.

On Foot. For walkers, Santa Fe is much safer than any large American city. However, in recent years there has been a disconcerting surge in late-night muggings on downtown streets. Police presence has been increased.

Vehicle traffic within Santa Fe is slow because of the narrow streets and congestion. Vehicle traffic on the highways practically everywhere in New Mexico is very fast, which is surprising considering the state's well-deserved reputation as one vast speed trap. The speed limit on I-25 between Albuquerque and Santa Fe recently was boosted to 75 miles per hour, but many still commute at 80-plus—on the theory that the State Police can't nail *everybody.* Be especially wary of speeding on Indian reservations, however: the posted highway speed limits are tortoise-slow (e.g., 35 mph), tribal police presence high, and pets and children likely to dart into the roadway. Radar detectors are legal in New Mexico and their employment is widespread.

Roadside services are few and far between off the main highways. (Underwood Archives, San Francisco)

■ DRESSING FOR SANTA FE

Now and then you'll see a woman strolling the streets of Santa Fe wearing: big triple-jointed Navajo turquoise earrings, a brilliant red-, yellow-, and blue-striped cotton blouse from Guatemala, three or four silver-and-turquoise bracelets, a silver concha belt encircling a long, full skirt, and medium heels. Beside her strides a well-manicured fellow wearing: cowboy boots, fringed jacket, big silver belt, and a turquoise Kokopelli on a thong around his neck.

Natives will point and snicker; Pueblo Indians will offer not only to sell them still more turquoise bracelets, but also a bridge over the Rio Grande Gorge.

The silliest thing you can do in Santa Fe is try to dress Santa Fe. Culturally, this is a very sophisticated city, but sartorially, it is studiously informal. Only one nose-in-air restaurant, The Compound, demands jackets for men. Even at the Santa Fe Opera the rule is no rule: "Anything goes," says press assistant Jackie Camborde. "We have people in tuxes and people in jeans and cowboy boots."

The one bit of sensible advice is to anticipate a wide range of temperatures. In summer, the nighttime mercury will almost always fall into the 50s.

Turquoise has been mined in New Mexico since prehistoric times.

An Hispanic girl poses in her fiesta finery in this hand-tinted photograph (opposite).

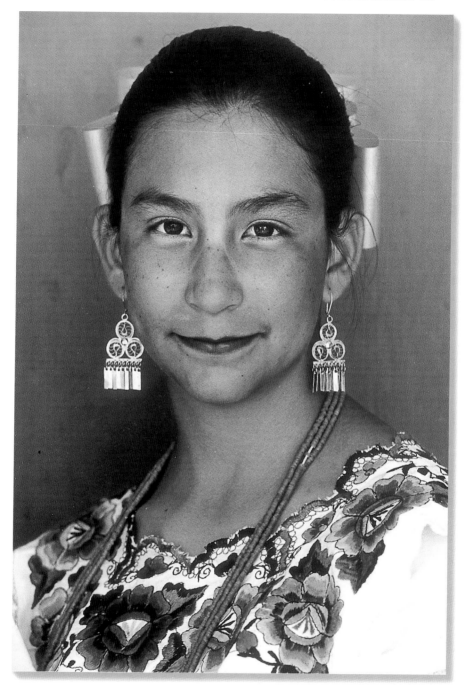

■ RESTAURANTS: See page 207.

■ LODGING: IN GENERAL

Santa Fe is *expensive*. No, *outrageous*. This is the first and absolutely accurate reaction of every cost-conscious visitor who tries to book a room and has his ears battered with a flurry of three-figure-a-night quotes.

Santa Fe is *full*. This is the dismayed realization of would-be July-through-September visitors who wait until the last few weeks to book reservations. Rooms during the opera season, Indian Market, or Albuquerque's Balloon Festival may seem unavailable at any price.

But there are almost always places to stay in Santa Fe—even sort of reasonably priced accommodations. Finding them takes personal initiative, not a travel agent. And well-in-advance planning is essential.

❖

Santa Fe accommodations fall into four basic categories: hotels, motels, B&Bs, and privately owned "vacation rentals."

Hotels. The hotels are clustered in or very near downtown, and all are upper-middle priced to very expensive. Happily, all cultivate a relaxed atmosphere, however stratospheric their rates. "We're informal even at dinner," said a clerk at the Inn of the Anasazi, which *Condé Nast Traveler* named one of the top 25 resorts in the country in 1996. "We might discourage a Metallica T-shirt." A powerful argument for staying in a hotel is that you'll have a parking space downtown.

Motels. Most of the motels line Cerrillos Road, the unromantic commercial strip that arrows several miles south from the central city. Traffic on Cerrillos is unbelievable in summer, and driving downtown to find parking—well, head out at 7 A.M. But the price differential is substantial. In a recent summer survey the New Mexico Hotel and Motel Association found the average daily rate for a hotel room in downtown 87 percent higher than the average room on Cerrillos Road.

B&Bs. Bed & breakfasts are a blooming cottage industry in Santa Fe; there are at least 30 in operation at this writing. Nearly all operate in historic adobe or Victorian houses within walking distance of downtown, and most provide sumptuous, if late, breakfasts. Costs generally fall between Cerrillos motel and downtown hotel rates.

The Inn at Loretto is one of Santa Fe's most popular accommodations.

Rentals. Vacation rentals are often overlooked. Many Santa Fe residents rent out their homes or adjoining "casitas" for much of the year. Several local agencies specialize in booking the higher-priced rentals (i.e., $1,200–$3,000 per month). If you're looking for a better deal, an excellent investment is a one-month mail subscription to the *Santa Fe New Mexican*, (800) 873-3372. Not only will the news and cultural sections whet you for a visit to the city, but the "Vacation Rentals" heading in the classifieds can also lead to a quiet, comfortable place at a quasi-reasonable cost. Many vacation rentals are available by the day, week, or month.

In any event, it matters when you come. The "high season" at most places stretches from May 1 through October 31; rates at other times are 15 to 30 percent less. Some hotels kick their rates back up around Thanksgiving and Christmas, when Santa Fe again becomes a popular, if frosty, destination.

Also keep in mind that hotel, motel, and sometimes even B&B rates are negotiable in all but times of peak occupancy. If you're not a member of a discount plan (such as AAA, AARP, or Encore), ask for the corporate rate and describe your business in Santa Fe.

Reservations. If every place you call personally is booked up, try one of the several private reservation services:

New Mexico Central Reservations, (800) 466-7829 or (505) 766-9770

Santa Fe Central Reservations, (800) 776-7669 or (505) 983-8200

Bed & Breakfast of New Mexico, (505) 982-3332

Some visitors also stay in nearby towns and commute into Santa Fe. Española and Los Alamos are each an easy 30-mile drive, and their motels are substantially less expensive than Santa Fe's. Los Alamos is the more interesting city.

■ LODGING: LISTINGS

Chains. Many major hotel and motel chains are well-represented in Santa Fe. To find out what is available and where, use the national 800 numbers listed below, but for the best rates make your reservations at the local number; the reservations clerk is frequently authorized to quote discounted rates.

Best Western International. (800) 528-1234

Days Inn. (800) 329-7466

Hilton Hotels. (800) HILTONS

Holiday Inn. (800) HOLIDAY

Marriott Hotels. (800) 228-9290

Radisson. (800) 333-3333

Ramada Inn. (800) 2-RAMADA

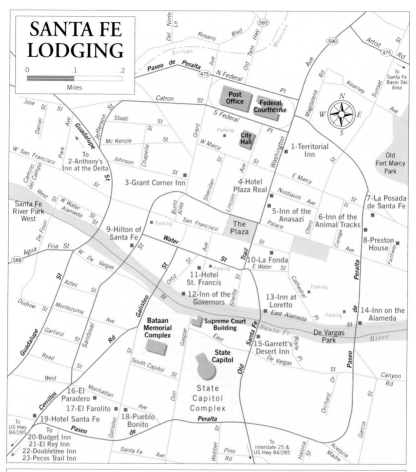

SANTA FE LODGING

> $\mathcal{P}$rice designations for lodging:
> $ = under $90; $$ = $90–$150; $$$ = $150–up

■ CENTRAL SANTA FE

Alexander's Inn. 529 E. Palace Ave.;
(505) 986-1431 $$
This Craftsman-style house built in 1903 has seven guest rooms, gardens, and a backyard hot tub. Short walk from the Plaza.

El Farolito. 514 Galisteo St.;
(505) 988-1631 $$
Seven adobe casitas with fireplaces and private baths. Charming Southwestern features including flagstone floors, exposed vigas, and skylights.

EL PARADERO

El Paradero. 220 W. Manhattan Ave.;
(505) 988-1177 $–$$
One of Santa Fe's first B&Bs, El Paradero remains among the most pleasant. Twelve rooms in a rambling 1800s adobe farmhouse remodeled in Territorial style. Fine breakfasts. Six blocks to the Plaza.

Garrett's Desert Inn. 311 Old Santa Fe Trail;
(800) 888-2145 or (505) 982-1851 $–$$
The architecture is strictly Motel Deco Plain-o, but rooms are very pleasant and freshly furnished—and these are the most affordable downtown digs you're going to find. Four blocks from the Plaza.

Grant Corner Inn. 122 Grant Ave.;
(505) 983-6678 $$
Surrounded by flower gardens and a picket fence, this Colonial-style B&B seems out of its element in Santa Fe. Only two blocks from the Plaza.

Hilton of Santa Fe. 100 Sandoval St.; (800) 336-3676 or (505) 988-2811 $$$
Conviently located for the business traveler. Staff speaks many languages. Santa Fe decor.

Hotel Plaza Real. 125 Washington Ave.;
(800) 279-7325 or (505) 988-4900 $$$
This small hotel features rooms that open onto a narrow brick courtyard brightened

HOTEL PLAZA REAL

with many flowers. Most have wood-burning fireplaces.

Hotel St. Francis. 210 Don Gaspar Ave.; (800) 529-5700 or (505) 983-5700 $$
This gracious Spanish Colonial Revival hotel was built in 1923, allowed to run down, and thoroughly renovated in 1986.

HOTEL ST. FRANCIS

Most rooms are still small by modern standards. Grand lobby and veranda, high tea served to guests every afternoon.

Hotel Santa Fe. 1501 Paseo de Peralta; (800) 825-9876 or (505) 982-1200 $$–$$$
A little farther from the Plaza (six blocks) and a little less expensive. This modern 131-room Pueblo Revival hotel has large, warmly decorated rooms and a free shuttle to downtown.

Inn at Loretto–Best Western. 211 Old Santa Fe Trail; (505) 988-5531 $$$
Adjacent to the Loretto Chapel, this five-storied Pueblo-style inn is decorated with handmade furnishings and Native American artwork. Reasonably priced for the location; includes a swimming pool and restaurant.

Inn of the Anasazi. 113 Washington Ave.; (800) 688-8100 or (505) 988-3030. $$$
A beautiful and very expensive small hotel that opened in 1991 and met resounding acclaim. All rooms have gas fireplaces and ceilings of *vigas* and *latillas*. Don't expect views; all 59 rooms are squeezed into a long, narrow downtown block between another hotel and a burrito shop.

Inn of the Animal Tracks. 707 Paseo de Peralta; (505) 988-1546 $$
Five rooms in a delightful restored adobe four blocks from the Plaza. A warm staff and an inviting, cozy atmosphere. Each room is whimsically decorated after a different animal—the "soaring eagle," the "loyal wolf," etc. Always changing, always savory breakfasts.

INN OF THE ANIMAL TRACKS

Inn of the Governors. 234 Don Gaspar Ave.;
  (800) 234-4534 or (505) 982-4333
  $$–$$$
A downtown motel three blocks south of
the Plaza. The better rooms have wood-
burning fireplaces.

INN ON THE ALAMEDA

Inn on the Alameda. 303 E. Alameda St.;
  (800) 289-2122 or (505) 984-2121 $$$
An intimate 66-room hotel by the linear
River Park four blocks east of the Plaza.
"Breakfast of Enchantment" buffet includ-
ed. Some rooms with fireplaces and views.

La Fonda. 100 E. San Francisco St.;
  (800) 523-5002 or (505) 982-5511 $$$
Kennedy slept here, as did Errol Flynn,
Raymond Burr, and Diane Keaton. More
to the point for modern guests, each room
and most of the public spaces have been
graced with murals or painted furnishings
by Ernest Martinez, La Fonda's resident
artist for 40 years. A grand and comfortable
hotel whose tapestry of art, architecture,
and history makes it worth the price.

LA POSADA DE SANTA FE

La Posada de Santa Fe. 330 E. Palace Ave.;
  (800) 727-5276 or (505) 986-0000
  $$–$$$
Parts of this famous inn date from the
1930s; today 119 rooms of varying styles
and decor sprawl across six acres of gracious
but not fussy landscaping. Some rooms feature Southwestern decor, some Victorian.
Ask about views; the cheaper rooms overlook parking lots.

Preston House B&B. 106 Faithway St.;
  (505) 982-3465 $$–$$$
A 15-room Queen Anne Victorian built in
1886. Serene gardens, stained glass windows, lace curtains, and in-house masseuse.
Sherry and fruit bowl await every guest.

Pueblo Bonito. 138 W. Manhattan Ave.;
  (505) 984-8001 $$
Narrow brick paths wind below adobe
archways and huge shade trees on the
grounds of this century-old adobe com-
pound. Old Santa Fe-style furnishings
combined with modern local artwork.

Territorial Inn. 215 Washington Ave.; (505) 989-7737. $$–$$$
This quiet B&B is set back from the street by large cottonwood trees. Built by a wealthy Philadelphian around the turn of the century, the house has a long history of lavish parties and gracious owners. Rose garden and hot tub.

■ **G R E A T E R S A N T A F E**
Besides the following listings, most of the major motel chains have places on Cerrillos Road, including Holiday Inn, Howard Johnson, La Quinta Inn, Motel 6, Park Inn, Ramada Inn, Travelodge.

Bishop's Lodge. Bishops Lodge Rd. off NM 590, 3 miles north of Santa Fe; (800) 732-2240 or 983-6377. $$$
This luxury resort began as an unpretentious mountain retreat for Bishop Lamy, who bought the property for $80 sometime in the 1860s. Operated as a resort by the Thorpe family since 1918, it now features

BISHOP'S LODGE

88 rooms, a restaurant, horseback riding, tennis, and a seven-day-a-week summer children's program to keep youngsters occupied. Quiet, forested, beautiful views.
Budget Inn. 725 Cerrillos Rd.; 982-5952. $
AAA, free breakfast from Monroe's New Mexican Food (adjacent) with room. Walking distance to downtown.
Doubletree Inn. 3347 Cerrillos Rd.; (505) 222-8733 or (800) 777-3347. $$
A sprawling motel with 211 rooms, all with fridges and wet bars. Indoor pool.

EL REY INN

El Rey Inn. 1862 Cerrillos Rd.; (800) 521-1349 or 982-1931. $–$$
More than a basic motel, guest rooms are beautifully decorated in Pueblo, Spanish, or Victorian styles. Many have fireplaces. A good value.
Pecos Trail Inn. 2239 Old Pecos Trail; 982-1943. $
Good location two miles from downtown but away from the visual blight of Cerrillos Road. Large rooms, some with kitchenettes. A good value.

■ B E Y O N D   S A N T A   F E

Particularly in summer, some visitors pass up Santa Fe's costs and crowds and stay in a smaller nearby town such as Española (28 miles) or Los Alamos (35 miles). Contact the **Española Valley Chamber of Commerce and Visitor Information Center,** (505) 753-2831; or the **Los Alamos County Chamber of Commerce,** (505) 662-8105. In Taos, try the **Taos County Chamber of Commerce,** (505) 758-3873 or (800) 732-8267; or the **Taos B&B Association,** (505) 758-4747 or (800) 876-7857.

Anthony's Inn at the Delta. 304 Paseo de Oñate, Española, 25 miles north of Santa Fe; (505) 753-9466 $$

A beautiful new B&B with vast rooms, kiva fireplaces, jacuzzi tubs, and furniture by Santa Fe artisans. Rooms like this would cost $250/day in Santa Fe—if they existed.

Hacienda Vargas. Thirty miles south of Santa Fe on I-25, exit Algodones, left on NM 313; (800) 261-0006 or (505) 867-9115 $$-$$$

HACIENDA VARGAS

A stagecoach stop in the late 1700s, an Indian trading post in the 1900s, and today, a cozy B&B. All seven guest rooms have kiva fireplaces, antique furnishings, and contemporary Southwest art. Friendly staff, pleasant garden and courtyard.

RANCHO ENCANTADO

Rancho Encantado. Rte. 4, off State Rd 592 in Tesuque, 8 miles north of Santa Fe; (800) 722-9339 or (505) 982-3537 $$$

Few accommodations offer more spectacular views. Sprawled across 168 acres above the stunning Rio Grande Valley, the resort attracts celebrity guests from Robert Redford to the Dalai Lama.

Ten Thousand Waves. Hyde Park Rd., 3.5 miles north of Santa Fe; (505) 982-9304 $$$

A unique Japanese-style health spa offering private and communal hot tubs outdoors xthe woods, massage therapy, herbal wraps, and three luxury cabins for overnighters. Especially popular with sore skiers returning from the mountains.

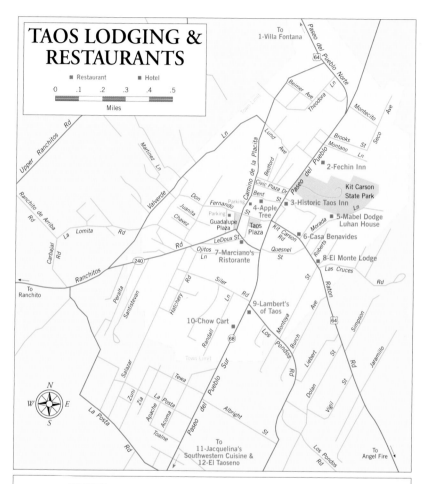

TAOS LODGING & RESTAURANTS

■ Restaurant   ■ Hotel

0   .1   .2   .3   .4   .5
Miles

LODGING	RESTAURANTS
Casa Benavides 6	Apple Tree 4
El Monte Lodge 8	Chow Cart 10
Fechin Inn 2	El Taoseno 12
Mabel Dodge Luhan House 5	Lambert's of Taos 9
Historic Taos Inn 3	Marciano's Ristorante 7
	Jacquelina's Southwestern Cuisine 11
	Villa Fontana 1

■ C H I M A Y Ó

Hacienda Rancho de Chimayó. Santa Fe County Rd., off NM 503; (505) 351-2222 $–$$

A lovely B&B across the road from the famous Restaurante Rancho de Chimayó. Seven rooms in an old adobe hacienda surround a courtyard. Much peace and quiet. About 40 miles north of Santa Fe.

HACIENDA RANCHO DE CHIMAYO

■ T A O S

Casa Benavides. 137 Kit Carson Rd.; (505) 758-1772 $$–$$$

A modern and colorful B&B. Navajo rugs, Native American pottery, flagstone floors, and other Southwestern trappings adorn the spacious rooms.

El Monte Lodge. 317 Kit Carson Rd.; (800) 828-8267 or (505) 758-3171 $–$$

An old but very nicely maintained mom 'n' pop motel near downtown. Quiet, spacious rooms, some with beehive fireplaces or kitchens.

Fechin Inn. 227 Paseo del Pueblo Norte; (505) 751-1000 $$$

This elegant hotel embraces the Russian artist Nikolai Fechin's home physically as well as spiritually; the lobby furniture is hand-carved in Fechin's distinctively rustic style.

Mabel Dodge Luhan House. 240 Morada Ln.; (505) 758-9456 $$$

Early in the century, Mrs. Luhan coaxed many literati, including D. H. Lawrence and Willa Cather, to come West and stay in her rambling, old house. Even in it's present incarnate as an 11-room B&B the artistic tradition continues with frequently held workshops and writers' conferences. There's a casual, rather rustic flavor to the place.

Historic Taos Inn. 125 Paseo del Pueblo Norte; (800) 826-7466 or (505) 758-2233 $$$

Taos's famous old downtown hotel opened in 1936, but parts of the building date from the 1600s. Most rooms have fireplaces. Much local art on display.

HISTORIC TAOS INN

The dining room at the Mabel Dodge Luhan House

■ MUSEUMS

■ SANTA FE

Center for Contemporary Arts of Santa Fe. 291 E. Barcelona Rd.; (505) 982-1338. Provocative visual arts. (See p. 89)

El Rancho de las Golondrinas. 334 Los Pinos Rd. (15 miles south of Santa Fe); (505) 471-2261. A living-history museum of Spanish Colonial culture.

Georgia O'Keeffe Museum. 217 Johnson St.; (505) 995-0785. A new museum devoted exclusively to New Mexico's most celebrated artist. (See p. 91)

Institute of American Indian Arts Museum. 108 Cathedral Pl.; (505) 988-6281. (See p. 91)

Museum of Fine Arts. 107 W. Palace Ave.; (505) 827-4455. Twentieth-century New Mexican art, including a permanent exhibit of works by Georgia O'Keeffe. (See p. 91)

Museum of Indian Arts and Culture. 710 Camino Lejo; (505) 827-6344. Pottery from eleventh-century Anasazi to contemporary Pueblo and Navajo artisans. (See p. 92)

Museum of International Folk Art. 706 Camino Lejo; (505) 827-6350. (See p. 92)

Palace of the Governors. Palace Ave., north side of the Plaza; (505) 827-6474. New Mexican history exhibits including Spanish and American colonial life. (See pps. 104–105)

Santa Fe Children's Museum. 1050 Old Pecos Trail; (505) 989-8359. A private, non-profit museum with hands-on displays in the arts, sciences, and history.

Wheelwright Museum of the American Indian. 704 Camino Lejo; (505) 982-4636. Changing exhibits feature contemporary art by Native American artists. (See p. 92)

■ TAOS

Ernest Blumenschein Home and Museum. 222 Ledoux St.; (505) 758-0505. Paintings by Taos art colony founder Ernest Blumenschein and other Taos artists. (See p. 137)

Fechin Institute. 227 Paseo del Pueblo Norte; (505) 758-1710. Hand-carved woodwork and furnishings, Russian and Spanish folk art, and Oriental art. (See p. 136)

Governor Bent House and Museum. 117-A Bent St., 1 block north of the Plaza; (505) 758-2376. American frontier memorabilia and furnishings. (See p. 136).

Harwood Foundation Museum. 238 Ledoux St.; (505) 758-9826. Paintings, drawings, photographs, and sculpture from the earliest years of Taos as an art colony. (See p. 137)

Kit Carson Home and Museum. Kit Carson Rd., half a block east of Taos Plaza; (505) 758-0505. (See pps. 136)

Martinez Hacienda. Ranchitos Rd. (NM 240), 2 miles south of Taos Plaza; 758-0505. Adobe house with 21 rooms furnished in original Spanish Colonial style. (See pages 137–138)

Millicent Rogers Museum. Millicent Rogers Museum Rd., 4 miles north of the Plaza off NM 522; 758-2462. Pueblo and Navajo jewelry, textiles, and pottery. (See page 137)

Van Vechten–Lineberry Taos Art Museum. 501 N. Pueblo Rd.; (505) 758-2690. Private museum showcasing the work of Duane Van Vechten. (See p. 137)

The bedroom of the Ernest Blumenschein House (opposite).

(preceding pages) The kitchen at Martinez Hacienda.

■ OUTDOORS

With more than 300 days of sunshine a year and usually mild weather, northern New Mexico begs for outdoor recreation of all sorts. One caveat: Santa Fe and Taos both lie at around 7,000 feet, so don't expect to replicate the level of strenuous activity you're accustomed to in the lowlands.

■ HIKING

Scores of maintained hiking trails wind through the deserts and forests around Santa Fe; the sheer variety of scenery is astounding. A useful guide, available at many Santa Fe bookstores, is *Day Hikes in the Santa Fe Area,* published by the Santa Fe Group of the Sierra Club. The club, a gregarious and thoroughly pleasant bunch, usually schedules two or three-day hikes every weekend, and visitors are always welcomed whether Sierra Clubbers or not. Check the left-hand column on the first page of the *Santa Fe New Mexican*'s Outdoors section every Thursday for announcements.

When hiking in New Mexico, be careful of overexertion and overexposure to sun (always apply a sunscreen). Rattlesnakes are, well, out there, but are easy to avoid. Don't put hands or feet anywhere you haven't looked, don't sit down to rest on a rock or log without looking around it, and never, ever torment a snake. Veteran hikers in the Southwest swear to this aphorism: Don't be the third hiker in a group. Why? "The first one wakes the snake up, the second one ticks him off, and the third one gets the fangs." They're just kidding—probably.

The forests around Santa Fe also are home to a fair number of black bears. Avoiding trouble is mostly a matter of knowing what *not* to do:

① Don't panic—you won't remember the rest of these rules.
② Don't run. It triggers the bear's chase instinct, and bears can easily outrun people.
③ Don't climb a tree. Black bears, unlike grizzlies, are terrific climbers.
④ Don't lie down and play dead.
⑤ Don't throw anything, shout, or growl at it.

Just back slowly away, keeping a wary eye on the bear but not trying to stare it down, which could be interpreted as a contest for dominance.

If the bear charges anyway, you probably still don't need a Plan B. Usually it will be a bluff charge. If not, well, there really isn't a Plan B.

Lost again in the Bisti Badlands.

■ SKIING

Northern New Mexico sports eight ski areas within two hours' drive of Santa Fe, an embarrassment of slippery riches if ever there were one. Taos Ski Valley is the undisputed king, a world-class mountain rated second in challenge among American ski resorts by readers of *Ski* magazine. Santa Fe Ski Area, only 16 miles from town, offers a wider range of beginner, intermediate, and advanced slopes, and spectator events such as the January Celebrity Ski Classic.

The ski areas peak at 12,000 to 13,000 feet and average 110 to 350 inches of snow every year. Yet the weather is unlikely to be bitterly cold; meteorologists calculate the chance of skiing under sunlight to be 70 to 80 percent on a given day. The ski season, on average, stretches from the third week of November into late April. Most of the areas, Taos in particular, have nearby accommodations to offer.

Road conditions statewide are available from the New Mexico State Police at (505) 827-5594. Ski packages, including transportation, accommodations and ski tickets, can be booked through New Mexico Central Reservations, (800) 4NM-STAY or within New Mexico, (505) 766-9770.

NORTHERN NEW MEXICO SKI RESORTS

Ski Area	Area Phone	Snow Phone	Peak Elev.	Avg. Snowfall	Runs
Angel Fire	(800) 633-7463	(505) 377-4222	10,650'	210"	58
Pajarito	(505) 662-5725	(505) 662-7669	10,441'	140"	37
Red River	(505) 754-2223	(900) 468-7669	10,350'	214"	58
Sandia	(505) 242-9133	(505) 242-9052	10,378'	125"	28
Santa Fe	(505) 982-4429	(505) 857-8977	12,000'	225"	38
Sipapu	(505) 587-2240	(505) 587-2240	9,065'	110"	19
Ski Rio	(800) 227-5746	(800) 227-5746	11,650'	250"+	64
Taos	(505) 776-2291	(505) 776-2916	11,819'	320"+	72

The ski basin above Santa Fe is only a 30-minute drive from the Plaza.

■ R A F T I N G

The brochure of one of several Taos- and Santa Fe-based river rafting companies begins thus:

Our full-day Taos Box trip, on the Rio Grande Wild and Scenic River, traverses 16 miles of wilderness gorge, encountering demanding rapids guaranteed to get you wet. This, our most exciting trip, is NOT for the timid.

Watching the Big River wind its stately course through gardens of great cottonwoods beside NM 68 south of Taos, it's hard to envision the thrills—or terrors—of Class IV rapids a few miles upstream—but they're there, at least in the Rocky Mountains' spring runoff season. Not all the rafting trips are reserved only for the intrepid, however. Many others are placid, pastoral recreational floats, some also featuring fishing, visits to petroglyph sites, or twilight dinner on the riverbank. For the most part, the rafting season stretches from April to October. Whitewater enthusiasts will most appreciate April, May, and June. However, if you do go rafting don't be surprised if you get dirty looks from the locals. The locals are trying to create "rafter-less days" so the Rio Grande can return to normal.

To get wet on the Rio Grande or the smaller Rio Chama, check the Santa Fe or Taos yellow pages under "River Trips." A sampling:

Santa Fe Rafting Company. (800) 467-7238 or (505) 988-4914.

New Wave Rafting Company. Santa Fe, (800) 984-1444 or (505) 984-1444.

Los Rios River Runners. Taos, (800) 544-1181 or (505) 776-8854.

■ G O L F I N G

Santa Fe offers one public golf course, **Santa Fe Country Club**, Airport Rd.; (505) 471-0601.

Cochiti Lake, 25 miles to the southwest off NM 22, has an 18-hole course rated in *Golf Digest's* Top 25, (505) 465-2239.

■ TOURS

Walking tours, flying tours, historic church tours, pueblo tours—all are available in Santa Fe, and given the richness and complexity of northern New Mexico's culture and history, an expert's guidance can be very helpful. Reservations should always be made. A sampling of tours:

Aboot About/Santa Fe Walks. Two-hour walking tours of downtown Santa Fe, led by opinionated local historians and ghost tours in the evening. (505) 988-2774.

Afoot in Santa Fe Riding Tours. These short (75-minute) open-air tram tours depart from the downtown Inn at Loretto and cover central Santa Fe's most important significant landmarks. (505) 983-3701.

Pueblos del Norte Nambé Tours. Day-long tours to Nambé, Pojoaque, Picurís, San Juan, San Ildefonso, Santa Clara, and Taos, conducted by Indian guides. Special visits to feast days. (505) 820-1340.

Rocky Mountain Tours. This versatile company offers balloon flights over Santa Fe and Albuquerque, horseback rides out of Santa Fe and Taos, and charter aircraft tours of the Santa Fe area. (505) 984-1684.

New Mexico Mountain Bike Adventures. Guides trained in first aid lead half-day, full-day, and overnight adventures into the Jémez Mountains and northern New Mexico ghost towns. (505) 264-5888.

■ FESTIVALS

It's difficult to visit northern New Mexico at a time when there isn't some sort of festival going on. The Santa Fe Opera season is perhaps the best known, but Indian Market draws the largest crowds—more than 100,000 lookers and shoppers. For schedules contact the local Convention and Visitors Bureaus (see page 251). Most of the pueblos have feast days and dances that are open to the public. For dates, call the Eight Northern Indian Pueblos Council at (505) 852-4265.

JANUARY
All Kings Day. Various dances at most northern pueblos. (800) 793-4955.
New Mexican Wine Tasting. Taos Ski Valley. (505) 776-2291.
Super Ski Week. Taos Ski Valley. (505) 776-2291.

FEBRUARY
Santa Fe: Winter Fiesta. Snow-sculpture competitions, racing clinics, and obstacle ski races. (800) 776-SNOW.

Music and dance are a feature of all Hispanic celebrations. These photos (above and opposite) are from one of the many festivals celebrated at Rancho de las Golondrinas, a living-history museum 15 miles south of Santa Fe.

MAY

Taos: Spring Arts Celebration. Several performances and events including the Spring Art Show, the Taos Community Chorus, Orchestra Spring Concert, Taos Art Auction, artisans' festival, and "Art in the Park for Kids." (505) 758-3873 or (800) 732-8267.

JUNE

Taos School of Music Summer Chamber Music Festival. June–August. 360 State Rd.; (505) 776-2388.

JULY

Behind Adobe Walls. Home tours. (505) 983-6565.

Contemporary Hispanic Market. Part of the traditional Spanish Market, this art festival features work by contemporary Hispanic artisans. (505) 988-1878.

Santa Fe Opera. July–August. P.O. Box 2408, Santa Fe 87504; (505) 986-5900.

Santa Fe Chamber Music Festival. July–August. 239 Johnson St., Santa Fe 87501. Box office (505) 982-1890.

Santa Fe Rodeo. (505) 471-4300.

Spanish Market. Traditional Spanish Colonial arts such as *santos* and carved furniture. Sponsored by the Spanish Colonial Arts Society; (505) 983-4038.

Taos Pueblo Powwow. Colorful dances performed by Native Americans from many tribes. (505) 758-9593.

AUGUST

Indian Market. Tribes from all over the country attend this two-day event at the Santa Fe Plaza. Dance performances and arts festival. Sponsored by Southwest Association for Indian Arts; (505) 983-5220.

Santa Fe Trail Anniversary. Palace of the Governors. (505) 473-3124.

SEPTEMBER

Fiestas de Santa Fe. Established in 1712 to commemorate the reconquest of Santa Fe by Don Diego de Vargas in 1692. Highlight is the ceremonial burning of Zozobra, Old Man Gloom. (505) 988-7575.

Taos Arts Festival. (800) 732-8267 or (505) 758-3873.

Wine and Chile Fiesta. (505) 982-9168.

DECEMBER

Winter Market. A smaller affair than the summer's Spanish Market but still the same idea: Spanish Colonial artwork, furniture, crafts. 983-4038

Yuletide in Taos. *Farolitos* tours, arts and crafts fair, dance performances, ski area activities. (800) 732-8267 or (505) 758-3873.

SMOKING CIGARS AT A BALL

Susan Shelby Magoffin left her native Kentucky in 1846 as an eighteen-year-old bride and set out for Santa Fe and Mexico on a trading expedition with her husband Samuel Magoffin and his brother James. The Magoffin brothers had been trading in the Southwest for nearly two decades, establishing themselves as well-known figures in the Mexican-ruled territory. In 1846, however, James Magoffin undertook the journey with more political intentions; he had secret instructions from President James Polk to negotiate Governor Armijo's peaceful surrender of New Mexico. As a member of this influential party, Susan Magoffin recorded her impressions of the fledgling Santa Fe society during the time of the American conquest.

Friday 11th [September 1846]

First the ballroom, the walls of which were hung and fancifully decorated with the "stripes and stars," was opened to my view—there were before me numerous objects of the biped species, dressed in the seven rain-bow colours variously contrasted, and in fashions adapted to the reign of King Henry VIII, or of the great queen Elizabeth, *my memory* cannot exactly tell me which, they were entirely enveloped, on the first view in a cloud of smoke, and while some were circling in a mazy dance others were seated around the room next the wall enjoying the scene before them, and quietly puffing, both males and females their little cigarritas a delicate cigar made with a very little tobacco rolled in a corn shuck or bit of paper. I had not been seated more than fifteen minutes before Maj. Soards an officer, a man of quick perception, irony, sarcasm, and wit, came up to me in true Mexican style, and with a polite, "Madam will you have a cigarita," drew from one pocket a *handfull of shucks and from an other a large horn of tobacco,* at once turning the whole thing to a burlesque.

—Susan Shelby Magoffin, *Down the Santa Fé Trail and into Mexico,* written 1846–47, published in 1926

■ INFORMATION NUMBERS

As telephone numbers and addresses frequently change, contact the local visitors' center for the most up-to-date information:

Santa Fe Convention and Visitors Bureau. P.O. Box 909, Santa Fe 87504; (505) 984-6760 or (800) 777-2489.

Taos County Chamber of Commerce. P.O. Drawer 1, Taos 87571; (505) 758-3873 or (800) 732-8267.

Los Alamos County Chamber of Commerce. P.O. Box 460, Los Alamos 87544; (505) 662-8105 or (800) 732-8267.

The end of the line . . .

New Mexico is famous for its spectacular sunsets.

RECOMMENDED READING

PERIODICALS

The *Santa Fe New Mexican* has been published continuously since 1849, which makes it the West's oldest newspaper. Its reporting is mainstream and its commentary fairly tepid, but it does a solid job of reporting Santa Fe's local news and ever-intriguing New Mexican politics. An outdoors section on Thursdays and *Pasatiempo,* an arts and entertainment tabloid on Fridays, are particularly useful to the visitor. Subscriptions: (800) 873-3372 or 984-0363.

Santa Fe Reporter, published Wednesdays, is Santa Fe's free "alternative" weekly. Its columnists are a good deal livelier and less predictable than the *New Mexican*'s. It, too, has comprehensive arts and entertainment coverage. Subscriptions: 132 E. Marcy, Santa Fe 87501; 988-5541.

Palacio, the excellent magazine of The Museum of New Mexico, has been published since 1895. Its authoritative and usually well-written articles deal in depth with New Mexican art, culture, history, and personalities. Subscriptions: P.O. Box 2087, Santa Fe 85704; 827-6451.

The *Santa Fean,* the slick local magazine, leans heavily towards arts coverage, naturally, but it also includes some quirky essays such as "Learning to Love Cerrillos Road." Subscriptions: 1440-A St. Francis Drive, Santa Fe 87505; (800) 835-3066.

New Mexico is the state-owned magazine published by the Tourism Department, where it's been a fixture since 1923. Coverage includes history, scenery, arts, and personalities throughout the state. Subscriptions: 495 Old Santa Fe Trail, Santa Fe 87501; 827-7447.

■ FICTION

Bradford, Richard. *Red Sky at Morning.* Philadelphia: Lippincott, 1968. A charming novel about a 17-year-old named Josh who spends World War II in a New Mexican town called Sagrado, which strongly resembles Taos.

Cather, Willa. *Death Comes for the Archbishop.* New York: Knopf, Inc., 1927. A thinly disguised and idealized historical novel about the life of Jean Baptiste Lamy. A classic and a good read, but had Cather acknowledged Lamy's flaws of character—he had a few—it would have been better.

La Farge, Oliver. *Behind the Mountains.* Los Angeles: Charles Publishing, 1984. The writing is elegant in this keenly detailed story of a family's life on a northern New Mexico sheep ranch.

Nichols, John. *The Milagro Beanfield War.* New York: Ballantine Books, 1976. A profound, brilliant, and funny novel about New Mexican Hispanic families rebelling against a rich gringo developer. All the humanity of *The Grapes of Wrath* and the fantasy of Marquez's *One Hundred Years of Solitude,* and more fun to read than either. Don't bother to rent the movie.

■ HISTORY

Benavides, Alonso de. *Benavides' Memorial of 1630.* Washington, DC: Academy of American Franciscan History, 1954. One of the few first-person accounts of Spanish Colonial New Mexico.

Gregg, Josiah. *The Commerce of the Prairies.* ed. by Max Moorhead. Norman: University of Oklahoma Press, 1954. The Santa Fe Trail seen through the eyes of a nineteenth-century trader.

La Farge, Oliver, and Arthur N. Morgan. *Santa Fe: Autobiography of a Southwestern Town.* Norman, OK: University of Oklahoma Press, 1985. Clippings from the *Santa Fe New Mexican* dating back to the newspaper's first edition in 1849.

Magoffin, Susan Shelby. *Down the Santa Fe Trail and into Mexico.* New Haven, CT: Yale University Press, 1926. The diary of Susan Shelby Magoffin, 1846–1847. A lively first-person account of the Southwest, its people and customs, during the American conquest of New Mexico.

Noble, David Grant. *Pueblos, Villages, Forts & Trails: A Guide to New Mexico's Past.* Albuquerque: University of New Mexico Press, 1994. A thick book of short articles, laced with historical anecdotes, on all the state's historic attractions—much more informative than the brochures handed out by the state parks, pueblos, and towns.

(following pages) The outrageous rock formations of the Bisti Badlands. The Navajos claimed this region as sacred burial land using the earth's natural colors as pigments for their sand paintings.

Noble, David Grant (editor). *Santa Fe: History of an Ancient City.* Santa Fe: School of American Research Press, 1989. One can never have too much Santa Fe history.

Old Santa Fe Today. Albuquerque: University of New Mexico Press, 1991. The Historic Santa Fe Foundation's well-documented and illustrated guide to Santa Fe's historic houses, churches, and plazas.

Simmons, Marc. *New Mexico: An Interpretive History.* Albuquerque: University of New Mexico Press, 1988. Simmons, a transplanted Texan, is New Mexico's most respected historian, and he writes in a bright, clear, non-academic voice.

Stuart, David E. *The Magic of Bandelier.* Santa Fe: Ancient City Press, 1989. Stuart, a University of New Mexico archaeologist, is one of the leading authorities on prehistoric New Mexico. This is a good, readable introduction to Bandelier and northern New Mexico prehistory.

■ COOKING

Dent, Huntley. *The Feast of Santa Fe.* New York: Simon and Schuster, 1985. If you buy only one Santa Fe cookbook, it should be this. No salmon-kumquat tacos here, just a thorough excursion through traditional New Mexican cooking.

■ ART

Cowart, Jack and Juan Hamilton, ed., *Georgia O'Keeffe: Art and Letters.* New York: New York Graphic Society Books, 1987. Chronicles the life and work of this celebrated artist.

Trimble, Stephen. *Talking with the Clay: the Art of Pueblo Pottery.* Santa Fe: School of American Research Press, 1987. Trimble is perhaps the most authoritative writer on Southwestern Native Americana today. This beautifully illustrated small book not only explains techniques and differences in pottery styles among Pueblo artists, but also explores their lives and their feelings toward their unique art.

■ ESSAYS AND MEMOIRS

Crawford, Stanley. *A Garlic Testament.* New York: HarperCollins, 1992. Crawford is an eloquent writer and a real-life garlic farmer in Dixon, 40 miles north of Santa Fe. This meditation on life, land, and garlic is engaging and luminous in its quiet wisdom.

Luhan, Mabel Dodge. *Edge of Taos Desert.* Albuquerque: University of New Mexico Press, 1987 (reprint of 1937 edition). In Taos Pueblo, the author, a disaffected New York sophisticate, discovers an idealized new world. "I finished it in a state of amazed revelation," testified her friend, Ansel Adams. Another Luhan title, *Lorenzo in Taos,* offers an amusing perspective of D. H. Lawrence.

Nichols, John. *If Mountains Die.* New York: Alfred A. Knopf, 1979. A Taos memoir by northern New Mexico's finest contemporary writer, bursting with love, outrage, and humor.

■ TRAVEL AND DESCRIPTION

Gabriel, Kathryn. *Roads to Center Place.* Boulder, CO: Johnson Publishing Company, 1991. If you've taken the recommended day trip to Chaco Canyon, this is the book that will help fill in some of the mysteries while still inspiring more questions—and probably more visits.

Hazen-Hammond, Susan. *Only in Santa Fe.* Stillwater, MN: Voyageur Press, 1992. This Hazen-Hammond book concentrates on contemporary Santa Fe—its quirks, its characters, its unique festivals. Wry, fun, but still informative. Eduardo Fuss's superb color photography illustrates everything from Santa Fe's flowers to the annual burning of the effigy of Zozobra, Old Man Gloom.

Preston, Douglas. *Cities of Gold.* New York: Simon & Schuster, 1992. An amazing chronicle of a Santa Fe author and his friend who try to retrace Coronado's route on modern horseback from the Mexican border to Pecos, New Mexico. History, adventure, and commentary weave together in a strong and seamless narrative.

G L O S S A R Y

Spanish words abound on northern New Mexico's maps, menus, street signs, and in everyday conversations—even among Anglos. An ordinary Spanish-English dictionary is not of much help because so many of the words are uniquely New Mexican. Bookstores have dictionaries of regional Spanish. Here is a guide to some of the more common *palabras de Nuevo Mexico.*

■ FOOD

Many Santa Fe menus provide helpful explanations of each dish. When you're marooned with one that doesn't . . .

carne adovada Literally "cured meat." A pork stew marinated in red chile sauce for 24 hours, then simmered in the same sauce. Pronounced "car-NEH ah-do-VAH-dah."

chiles rellenos Mild to moderately hot Hatch chiles stuffed with cheese, coated with egg batter, then fried in lard or oil. Pronounced "CHEE-lehs ray-YE-nos."

enchiladas Corn tortillas stuffed with cheese or meat, bathed in red or green chile sauce, and baked.

fajitas Literally "little skirts." Originally a Mexican stir-fry of onions, chiles, and thin strips of skirt steak, this now can be made with chicken, seafood, and even tofu. Pronounced "fa-HEE-tahs."

frijoles Beans, usually pinto or black. Frequently served as *frijoles refritos* (refried beans), where the boiled beans are mashed into a soft paste and cooked in

hot lard or oil. Pronounced "free-HO-lehs."

guacamole A dip made of mashed avocado, onion, garlic, tomato and spices. Pronounced "wah-kah-MO-ley."

picadillo Finely chopped beef or pork, sautéed with chiles, spices and sometimes raisins and almonds. Pronounced "pee-cah-DEE-yo."

piñon The nut of a native New Mexican pine, which has a delicately sweet, smoky flavor. Pronounced "peen-YOHN."

posole Hominy, often cooked with salt pork or tripe and red or green chiles. The classic northern New Mexican side dish. Pronounced "po-ZO-ley."

salsa (Literally "sauce") May refer to the appetizer dip usually served with fried tortilla chips, or to the red or green, ladled over a burrito—or to a *salsa nueva* as sophisticated as anything French.

sopaipillas Common New Mexican dessert. Airy puffs of sugared white flour, deep-fried and served with honey. Occasionally served as a main course, filled with a meat stuffing—a perversion. Pronounced "so-pie-PEE-yas."

t a m a l e s Spiced meat (usually beef) and chile swaddled in corn *masa* (moist ground corn) and dried corn husks, then steamed. The singular is not tamale, but tamál.

t a c o s In chain restaurants, ground beef, lettuce, tomatoes, and cheese stuffed into a folded and crisp-fried tortilla shell. In traditional New Mexican cuisine, better quality spiced meat swaddled in a soft tortilla.

t o r t i l l a In New Mexico, the staff of life is a disc. Traditionally made from ground corn and salt and lightly fried. Flour tortillas are equally common today.

■ OTHER WORDS

a r r o y o A normally dry riverbed, subject to flash flooding.

f a r o l i t o s Candles or electric lights placed in paper sacks and used to outline walkways, ledges, and rooftops during the Christmas season. Literally, "little lanterns."

h o r n o An adobe oven, generally shaped like a beehive. Pronounced "OR-no." (Spanish H is silent.)

l a t i l l a s Small sticks used to fill in the spaces between the *vigas* in the ceiling of a traditional Santa Fe house.

n i c h o A nook in the wall of a traditional Santa Fe house, used to hold a *santo* or other art work.

p l a z a The central square or park around which Spanish and Mexican towns were built.

p o r t a l A porch-like extension from the front or sides of a Spanish or Territorial-era building.

p o s a d a Inn. Very common name for hotels, motels, and B&Bs in New Mexico.

r i o River.

r i s t r a A bunch of dried red chiles tied together, generally for inside or outside decoration. Literally, "string."

s a n t e r o A professional carver of *santos*. Fem. *santera*.

s a n t o An image of a Christian saint, traditionally carved in wood.

v i g a s Round wooden beams, usually of pine, that stretch across the entire length of a traditional Santa Fe building and support the roof. Normally left exposed to view inside and protrude through the wall outside. Frequently faked, non-functional stubs on the exteriors of modern Spanish-Pueblo Revival buildings.

I N D E X

Comments, suggestions, or updated information?
Please write:
Compass American Guides
5332 College Ave., Suite 201
Oakland, CA 94618

COMPASS AMERICAN GUIDES

Critics, Booksellers, and Travelers All Agree You're Lost Without a Compass.

Compass American Guides are compelling, full-color portraits of America for travelers who want to understand the soul of their destinations. In each guide, an accomplished local expert recounts history, culture, and useful information in a text rife with personal anecdotes and interesting details. Splendid four-color images by an area photographer bring the region or city to life.

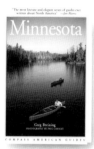

"This splendid series provides exactly the sort of historical and cultural detail about North American destinations that curious-minded travelers need."

—*Washington Post*

Boston (1st Edition)
1-878-867776-8
$18.95 ($26.50 Can)

"This is a series that constantly stuns us; our whole past book reviewer experience says no guide with photos this good should have writing this good. But it does."

—*New York Daily News*

Minnesota (1st Edition)
1-878-86776-8
$18.95 ($26.50 Can)

"Of the many guidebooks on the market few are as visually stimulating, as thoroughly researched or as lively written as the Compass American Guides series."

—*Chicago Tribune*

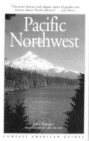

"Good to read ahead of time, then take along so you don't miss anything."

—*San Diego Magazine*

Pacific Northwest (1st Edition)
1-878-86785-7
$18.95 ($26.50 Can)

"Compass has developed a series with beautiful color photos and a descriptive text enlivened by literary excerpts from travel writers past and present."

—*Publishers Weekly*

Alaska (1st Edition)
1-878-86777-6
$18.95 ($26.50 Can)

Compass American Guides are available in general and travel bookstores, or may be ordered directly by calling (800) 733-3000. Compass American Guides are available at special discounts for bulk purchases for sales promotions or premiums. Special editions, including personalized covers and corporate imprints, can be created in large quantities for special needs. For more information, write to Special Marketing, Fodor's Travel Publications, 201 E. 50th St., New York, NY 10022; or call (800) 800-3246.

COMPASS AMERICAN GUIDES

Critics, Booksellers, and Travelers All Agree You're Lost Without a Compass.

Arizona (3rd Edition)
1-878-86772-5
$18.95 ($26.50 Can)

Chicago (2nd Edition)
1-878-86780-6
$18.95 ($26.50 Can)

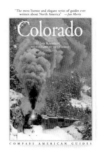

Colorado (3rd Edition)
1-878-86781-4
$18.95 ($26.50 Can)

Hawaii (3rd Edition)
1-878-86791-1
$18.95 ($26.50 Can)

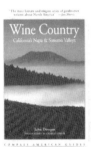

Wine Country (1st Edition)
1-878-86784-9
$18.95 ($26.50 Can)

Montana (3rd Edition)
1-878-86797-0
$18.95 ($26.50 Can)

Oregon (2nd Edition)
1-878-86788-1
$18.95 ($26.50 Can)

New Orleans (2nd Edition)
1-878-86786-5
$18.95 ($26.50 Can)

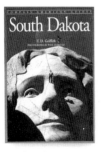

South Dakota (1st Edition)
1-878-86726-1
$16.95 ($22.95 Can)

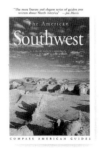

Southwest (1st Edition)
1-87866779-2
$18.95 ($26.50 Can)

Texas (1st Edition)
1-878-86764-4
$17.95 ($25.00 Can)

Utah (3rd Edition)
1-878-86773-3
$17.95 ($25.00 Can)

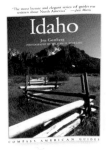

Idaho (1st Edition)
1-878-86778-4
$18.95 ($26.50 Can)

New Mexico (2nd Edition)
1-878-86783-0
$18.95 ($26.50 Can)

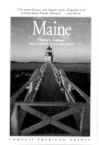

Maine (2nd Edition)
1-878-86796-2
$18.95 ($26.50 Can)

Manhattan (2nd Edition)
1-878-86794-6
$18.95 ($26.50 Can)

Las Vegas (4th Edition)
1-878-86782-2
$18.95 ($26.50 Can)

San Francisco (4th Edition)
1-878-86792-X
$18.95 ($26.50 Can)

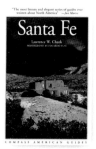

Santa Fe (1st Edition)
1-878-86775-X
$18.95 ($26.50 Can)

South Carolina (1st Edition)
1-878-86766-0
$18.95 ($26.50 Can)

Virginia (2nd Edition)
1-878-86795-4
$18.95 ($26.50 Can)

Washington (1st Edition)
1-878-86758-X
$17.95 ($25.00 Can)

Wisconsin (2nd Edition)
1-878-86749-0
$18.95 ($26.50 Can)

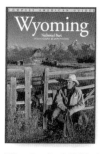

Wyoming (2nd Edition)
1-878-86750-4
$18.95 ($26.50 Can)

■ ABOUT THE AUTHOR

Lawrence W. Cheek has spent most of his life in the American Southwest. He has worked as a newspaper reporter, music and architecture critic, and editor for 17 years, and has taught journalism at the University of Arizona. As a freelance writer for the last several years, he has produced six books, including Compass American Guides' *Arizona*. His journalistic specialties are American architecture, Southwestern archaeology, and food.

■ ABOUT THE PHOTOGRAPHER

Eduardo Fuss was born in Buenos Aires and has lived in New Mexico since 1980. His photographs have appeared in *Smithsonian,* the *New York Times,* and *Arizona Highways,* among other publications, and have been featured exclusively in numerous books including *Hellish Relish* published by HarperCollinsWest, *Only in Santa Fe* published by Voyageur Press, and the award-winning *Chile Pepper Fever: Mine Is Hotter Than Yours,* also published by Voyageur Press.